The
Nanny Book

The
Nanny Book

The Smart Parent's Guide to Hiring, Firing, and Every Sticky Situation in Between

Susan Carlton and Coco Myers

 St. Martin's Griffin ✿ New York

THE NANNY BOOK: THE SMART PARENT'S GUIDE TO HIRING, FIRING, AND EVERY STICKY SITUATION IN BETWEEN. Copyright © 1999 by Susan Carlton and Coco Myers. All rights reserved. Printed in the United States of America. No part of this book may be used or reproduced in any manner whatsoever without written permission except in the case of brief quotations embodied in critical articles or reviews. For information address St. Martin's Press, 175 Fifth Avenue, New York, N.Y. 10010.

Design by Nancy Resnick

Library of Congress Cataloging-in-Publication Data

Carlton, Susan.
    The nanny book : the smart parent's guide to hiring, firing, and every sticky situation in between / Susan Carlton and Coco Myers.
        p. cm.
    ISBN 0-312-19933-3
    1. Nannies—Employment—United States—Handbooks, manuals, etc. I. Myers, Coco. II. Title.
HQ778.63.C365   1999
649—dc21   98-50583
                                        CIP

10 9 8 7 6 5 4 3

Contents

Preface

A little more than a year ago, we were talking on the phone—as usual—and somehow got on to the subject of nannies and whether Columbus Day counts as one of those must-give holidays. What if *you* don't get it off—what then? It got the two of us thinking—again—not only about that, but about the hundreds of caregiver conundrums we've grappled with while raising our kids (four between us, ages two to ten). We weren't the only ones wondering. It seemed that almost every parent we knew wanted corroboration that she, or he, was doing the right thing by her nanny, her kids, herself. We were all winging it, making up the rules of the house as we went along.

There ought to be a book, we thought, that you could turn to each time a question cropped up about how to conduct business, and friendship, with a nanny. (We mean "nanny" in the broadest and most contemporary sense: someone whose main responsibility is taking care of the children, whether she works part time or full time, lives in or out, and whether she's actually called "nanny," "caregiver," or "sitter"—terms we use interchangeably.) We envisioned a guide that dealt not only with the more pragmatic issues—from finding a nanny you can trust to negotiating salaries, raises, vacations, and overtime—but also with the real life, day-in, day-out ethics, such as whether it's kosher to ask the babysitter to pick up the dry cleaning or make the beds, what to do when a nanny's chronically late, whether a sitter should get paid more to supervise a play date. And, and, and . . .

Realizing that a book of this nature would have to be a mix of the objective and the subjective, we surveyed parents and caregivers across the country, gathering stories, advice, gripes, hearsay—anecdotes that got at the emotional underbelly of the relationship. We also tapped experts in various fields on boilerplate matters like immigration policy and the notorious nanny tax. Our goal was to get a consensus on as many ambiguous, complex, or touchy situations as we could, to provide a forum for comparing notes and a resource for finding advice and support. Each chapter starts with an overview in which we give our take on the topic at hand (be it discipline, divvying up duties, or coexisting under one roof), then moves on to a question-and-answer section that addresses very specific concerns. We also included in each chapter first-person accounts from parents, entitled "Overheard," and valuable insights from caregivers, dubbed "Nanny Point of View."

In the writing of this book it became clear that a nanny truly is part of the family framework, often a third and critical leg of a childrearing tripod. With any close-quarters relationship, however, there are going to be highs and lows, miscues and misunderstandings that need ironing out, and it's worth putting the effort into making the alliance strong, because the success of the parent–sitter dynamic really boils down to getting along. When everything's running smoothly and everyone's clicking, and you're confident your kids are in good hands, you feel your life is under control. And, as any parent knows, that goes a long way toward engendering peace of mind.

Acknowledgments

To the hundreds of friends, colleagues, nannies, and au pairs who shared their experiences, and tales of all kinds, and particularly to those who took the time to answer our lengthy survey (you know who you are), a million thanks. We're especially grateful to our girlfriends Karen Applebome, Judi Camps, Charlie Esposito, Laurette Kittle, Laura Marmor, Maura Rhodes, Louise Tutelian, and Karen Wood for their wisdom, humor, and optimism. And to Katherine Tasheff Carlton for her dedicated, smart, and skillful research assistance.

Our appreciation also to the many experts—agency owners, nanny trainers, au pair coordinators, lawyers, psychologists, accountants—who patiently answered our questions, particularly Elissa McGovern, American Immigration Lawyers Association; Jay Belsky, distinguished professor of human development, Pennsylvania State University; Stephanie Breedlove of Breedlove and Associates; Jimmye Walker of the United States Information Agency; Jeanne Salvatore of The Insurance Information Institute; Jacqueline Clark, A Choice Nanny; Claudia Kahn, The Help Agency; Lynn Peterson of PFC Information, a private investigative firm; Mary O'Connell, president, International Nanny

Association; Roberta Patterson, attorney and human resource consultant.

Thanks, too, to our editor, Hope Dellon, for her unwavering enthusiasm and her finely tuned ear for language; to her editorial assistant Maureen Drum, always available and helpful. And to our agent, Kim Witherspoon, who had faith in us and the project from the start.

Warmest thanks to our children, Annie and Jane Carlton and Max and Harrison Rowen—our biggest source of inspiration. And to our husbands, Ralph Carlton and Daniel Rowen, for their support and patience during our sometimes blindfold immersion in this book, and for their intelligent input. Last and foremost, we acknowledge the nannies in our lives, especially Glorita Bishop and Jackie Comic-Walker and Joby Weber, whose impact on our families and on this book has been great—in every sense of the word.

Part I

The Search

Chapter 1

Profile of a Perfect Sitter

So what are you looking for in a nanny? Who do you want walking through the door every morning or bustling about the kitchen when you wake up? The answer, hardly simple, is always loaded with expectations. We all have some version of the Mary Poppins icon rattling around in our heads—a person who's going to appear suddenly and magically instill order in our lives with the proper mix of authority, can-do energy, and charm. Can anyone really measure up? Still, we go on making our wish lists and creating our composite ideals: loving, nurturing, bright, cheerful, patient, dependable, loyal, unflappable—fill in the blanks.

In figuring out what sort of person you want to be around day after day, you have to make room for all your subjective preferences, including age and gender. You might, for example, gravitate toward someone older and more mature because you think she'll be maternal and loving (do you want some mothering yourself?). Then again, you might like the idea of a young nanny—someone you can groom and who can run with the job in every sense of the word. As for the male/female decision, most parents assume that a caregiver will, and should, be female; we associate babysitting with mother figures (in fact, we use the pronoun "her" throughout this book). But male nannies exist, albeit in small numbers, and on the face of it, there's no reason not to hire one— as long as you feel comfortable with the idea.

Plenty of parents have strong feelings about nannies' cultural backgrounds, too. Some relish the thought of an exotic influence; others don't want to deal with too many differences when it comes to childrearing customs, or even food. Then there are those employers who want only French- or Spanish-speaking sitters for the sake of hearing a second language in the house. A foreign language is definitely a plus if you want your kids to get their ears trained early, but it can also be a barrier to communication if the sitter's English is nonexistent and you have to resort to sign language. Most of us want a nanny who can at least read a bedtime story or understand a note with directions to a birthday party.

To flesh out the portrait of a perfect sitter, you have to factor in some practical considerations, like her life circumstances. Does the nanny have children of her own? Are they young and needy? If so, her flexibility—and consequently yours—may be limited by her outside responsibilities. Is she single, or settled down and settled in the neighborhood? A lot of parents believe that a married nanny is more emotionally stable and more likely to stick around than a free agent, though this theory doesn't take into account the fact that an unhappily married woman may be just as likely as the unmarried nanny to move on.

Once you've painted a broad brushstroke of your ideal, keep in mind that you're bound to have to compromise somewhere, on something. Focus on what matters most. If you end up interviewing a woman who's energetic and likeable, but a little too talkative, sit back and think about whether you could bear the chitchat for the sake of the enthusiasm. If, on the other hand, she's very quiet and shy but seems exceptionally warm, realize that while your kids will be nurtured, you probably won't get a lot of stimulating conversation (and you may end up being thankful for that). In the end you and the nanny have to get along.

You're going to be around each other—*a lot*—and in very intimate circumstances. Don't hold out for the great love affair, but do hold on to your standards.

WHO'S WHO IN THE WORLD OF NANNIES

Caregiver, babysitter, nanny—they are all defined as in-home childcare positions. But each has a different meaning, however subtle, and all are open to interpretation.

Nanny is by far the most popular, all-purpose name for someone who takes care of children, either as a live-in (she rooms and boards with the family, five or seven days a week) or as a live-out (she comes in on a daily basis). While the word "nanny" can conjure images of an English governess, the term is used much more broadly these days. It can describe a person who's had formal training in childcare (ranging from a degree in child development to intruction courses at a nanny college through an agency; or it can be used to describe a woman who's had on-the-job experience and has made a career out of taking care of kids.

Caregiver (or childcare provider or childcare technician) is an umbrella term that's more PC than it is catchy. While it's long been used by agencies and institutions, the word caregiver is only now being integrated into the childcare vernacular. Some parents gravitate toward the term because there's a neutrality about it; it sounds serious, and says what it is, without any elitist associations. Employees themselves often say they prefer it, though you rarely hear it used in nannies' conversation.

Babysitter (or sitter) covers a wide range of job descriptions. It can refer to someone who comes in on a Saturday night or a five-day-a-week regular employee. Agencies often eschew the term "babysitter," favoring "nanny" or "caregiver," because of the perception that no special training is required for the job of babysitter. Parents however, use "sitter" interchangeably with "nanny" and "caregiver"—in fact, many prefer it to "nanny," which to some still has the snooty ring of a servant for the upper classes.

Housekeeper for the most part means just what it implies—a person who cleans and takes care of the house. However, the job can spill over into babysitting and general care and feeding of the family—as in Alice on *The Brady Bunch*—particularly when the children are older and spend much of the day in school.

Au pair is in a category all its own. While it's a French term (meaning "on par" or "equal"), the au pair position has become a very American phenomenon. A legal au pair, anywhere from eighteen to twenty-six years old, comes from another country, and is hired through an official organization, under the auspices of the United States Information Agency. She lives with an American family for a year and gets a small weekly stipend. Motives for becoming an au pair include the desire to see the States, have an adventure, and maybe rechart one's future—which may or may not include childcare as a career.

American au pair is a variation on the foreign au pair. Major differences include the fact that these girls are not part of a government-sponsored cultural exchange program, there are no visa complications, and the fees, which aren't standardized, tend to be higher. There are similarities, too: The girls are young and eager to see a diffent place (in this case, another coast or a big city), and the stays with their host-families are usually short—a summer, or a year at most.

Baby nurse is defined as a specialist who cares specifically for newborns. These nurses move in, usually for two to three weeks—and then fly off to the next family. Their role is to train the first-time parents in such skills as breast feeding, bathing, caring for the umbilical cord, and nail cutting; or to give experienced parents a break so they can get some sleep—the same role mothers and grandmothers typically used to play. Most baby nurses are signed up with nanny agencies and may need to be reserved months in advance. They're the highest paid in the field, commanding double or triple an average nanny salary, and they see themselves as the highest rung on the childcare ladder.

TYPE CASTING

I've heard that hiring a nanny with her own young child is less than ideal, but I'd think her hands-on experience would be valuable.

This is a classic trade-off; what you gain in first-hand knowledge, you give up in flexibility. Someone with children of her own, especially preschoolers, often brings divided loyalties and energies. She may come in tired from being up late the night before with a teething infant or a nightmare-stricken toddler. Probably the biggest risk lies in her need to juggle her own childcare (to leave at a certain hour to pick up a kid at day care, to stay home when he's sick, or to miss work for doctor's appointments), which can hamper her ability to be available for you should you have to work late or travel (unless she's a live-in, in which case the point is moot). A nanny with a child at home doesn't necessarily present problems, however, if she has ever ready backup in the form of a husband, mother, sister. The motto here: The more complicated your life is, the less complicated you want hers to be. What works best for many families is a woman who has raised her own children and has seen them off to school or off on their own, or a non-mother who's come right off a job caring for a child the same age as yours—she's got the experience *and* the freedom.

In my work life I tend to hire go-getter types—the more ambitious the better—and that's my first impulse in looking for a

caregiver as well. But I wonder if it makes sense to apply the same thinking.

Some people like their nannies on the way up—they like being around those they perceive as bright and eager, and they like the role of mentoring a young nanny when it comes to her future. Certainly, ambitious types tend to do their jobs to the max, often exceeding expectations (so you do get your money's worth). But as in any work environment, ambition carries an obvious liability: The more enterprising a sitter is, the more likely she is to move on—and out of the job. Parents who have had bad luck with nannies quitting on them are more apt to look for someone who is committed to caregiving as a profession and isn't using baby-sitting as a stopgap.

AGE APPROPRIATE

I've always had this idea that when the time came to get a nanny, I'd want an older, grandmotherly type who was nurturing and gentle. It occurs to me I'm stuck on a stereotype.

A maternal, loving nature doesn't always come with age. It's possible that an older nanny might be a little worn out and have fewer reserves of affection than a less jaded sitter. But you won't ipso facto find high energy in a younger person either. These qualities are best judged on the spot in an interview. Stay open-minded: Just as some people lock onto an image of who they're going to marry, or where they'll live, or what their kids will look like, only to be surprised by what actually transpires, you can't predict what kind of nanny is going to spark your interest when she walks through the door.

I like the notion of a young, energetic nanny who can climb a tree with my four-year-old, but I worry about whether she'd be mature and wise enough to be a good all-around caregiver.

A twenty-something sitter is a pretty good playmate for a four-year-old, but while she may be able to jump and romp around, she may fall short in terms of patience, perspective, and resilience—that kids-will-be-kids attitude that's called for when your charming child throws a hysterical fit (or his shoes). Parents often find that younger nannies have a shorter fuse and are more apt to take personally a kid's fickle "I hate you." There are exceptions, of course—the very grown-up and savvy twenty-two-year-old, or the sitter who was raised as the oldest sibling in a large family, and for whom taking care of little kids is second nature. Where youth really does seem to be an advantage is with older kids—a twenty-five-year-old nanny who can still identify with the whims, moods and desires of a pre-adolescent can be like a big sister to a nine-year-old.

Overheard: Too Young, Too Much

We went to a local college in search of a part-time sitter for our three-year-old son. We didn't think we needed a real "nanny," just a playful but responsible young woman who would pick up our son at day care, give him a bath, and make him dinner before my husband and I came home from work. A lovely young freshman applied and we hired her on the spot. The first week on the job, she made a point of telling us how much fun she had with our son—that she had so much fun, in fact, she almost felt weird about being paid for it. The second week, she wrote us a letter about what a great family we were and how lucky she was to have landed this job. It was an absolute love fest—we were lucky, she was lucky, our son was lucky. And then, another two weeks went by and one night I came home to find her in a sullen mood. I asked her if everything was okay, and she nodded. I thought nothing more of it until my husband came home a few hours later and asked why *our son's car seat was sitting out in our driveway in the pouring rain. We went out to take a look, and there was the car seat we'd given the dream sitter to use in her car. Pinned on the buckle was a note. It just said, "Thank you for all your help, but I can no longer work for you." End of story. I immediately tried to call her and find out what the problem was, but the girls on her dorm floor were giving us the runaround. Finally, a week or so later, I did reach her, and she mumbled something about our son giving her a hard time one day and her parents wanting her to con-centrate on her studies. On reflection, my husband and I realized she was too immature to handle the workload, and that she didn't need the money badly enough to survive a difficult day.*

THE RIGHT CHEMISTRY

I tend to be a little scatterbrained and I have a lot going on in my life right now. I can't handle a nanny who's spacey, soft-spoken, or too needy. I want someone who can run the show.

Some parents consciously decide to hire somebody who will com-plement their own character—for example, a nanny who's force-ful and practical to balance their own indecisive, dreamy, insecure approach to life. Other parents gravitate to like-minded, like-spirited nannies, perhaps because they see them as exten-sion's of themselves. As for running the show, it's a good bet that an aggressive, assertive type is going to do a lot of the thinking, planning, deciding—for better and worse.

In the past I've had nannies with too much attitude, and we've clashed over everything from childrearing issues to how to put

the dishes in the dishwasher. I need a nanny who's comfortable following my lead.

There is no single description of a good soldier. While a strong-willed employer might not work well with a headstrong employee, the reverse isn't necessarily the solution either. You probably don't want to seek out a spineless, weak-willed sitter, since there will be times you'll *need* her to be in charge of the house and the kids, not to mention take action in an emergency. And it can be irritating to have someone always waiting for instructions or asking questions about whether she can do this or that. Unless you're a total control freak, it behooves you to try to find a middle ground—a nanny who is secure and professional enough to take the back seat without being a back-seat driver.

FOR APPEARANCES' SAKE

I'm a little embarrassed to admit that what a nanny looks and sounds like matters to me. I don't want to hire a nanny who's sloppy, obese, loud, or uneducated.

In many ways, the nanny is an ambassador of the family—she's with the child in public, day in and day out, whether she's picking him up at nursery school or play group, bringing him to the park, or taking him out to lunch. Some parents may feel that nannies who are friendly, outgoing, and well-spoken reflect well on them by association (and they often do: Other parents sometimes re-gard those sitters with a certain amount of envy). Of course, some parents care how *everything* around them looks—car, house, yard, kids, each other. Vanity aside, if there happen to be certain traits—physical or personal—that you can't tolerate, better to be honest with yourself and look for what you *do* like, otherwise you may find yourself irritated and begin picking on things that weren't really a problem in the first place.

A FOREIGN INFLUENCE

I'm thinking of hiring a personable young woman whose sister works for my neighbor. But her English is limited (she happens to be from Guatemala,) and I worry about how she'd be able to cope in an emergency, much less talk to me on a daily basis.

In many areas, 911 operators are bilingual, so in terms of a true emergency, her language skills needn't present much of a problem. Besides, even someone with full command of the English language can freeze and become totally mute under stress. The more critical criterion may be communication on a day-to-day basis. Think of all the things you need to get across to the sitter, from when to give the baby his ear-infection medicine to how you'd like them to spend the afternoon together. And what of reading books to the child? Plus, you want to be able to get feedback from her—her concerns or questions, stories of the day. Language, however, isn't always a total barrier to a good working relationship. A lot of parents and nannies get creative with symbols and hybrid words, and lots of loving relationships with kids have been nurtured with minimal English.

I like the idea of having a nanny who speaks a language in addition to English. I want my one-year-old to be exposed early. But there's a little piece of me that fears I'll be squeezed out of their private world.

True, you may be enchanted by your child's first words of French or Filipino, and, also true, you may feel a twinge of jealousy toward the nanny for having a link with the child that you don't have. But foreign language or no, you have to realize that a nanny and child will construct their own way of communicating anyway: words they make up, phrases they pick up from a book they read— a shared frame of reference that is by nature exclusive. And often the sitter, who is around all day long, becomes the main translator of a preverbal toddler's gibberish. Just be glad for the input—and the instruction.

Overheard: Caribbean Blues

A number of my friends have hired sitters from the Caribbean, many of whom have left their own children behind in the islands. The whole idea of endorsing this kind of family separation by being an employer made me uncomfortable. I couldn't imagine leaving my own children for any reason. So how painful, I thought, must it be for these women to live here alone and see their kids only once a year, if that. I worried, too, that this kind of nanny might be less than perfect in terms of how much she might be willing to give if she harbored the slightest bit of resentment toward an intact family. But when it came time for me to hire a nanny for my five-month-old, of all the woman I interviewed, the one I liked the most happened to be from Barbados, and happened to have a son and daughter, ages five and ten, living with her sister back home. I hired her hoping that I would be able to get past my own strange mix of guilt and disapproval. What helped was how genuinely cheerful she was most of the time. Her only bad days, or bouts of blues, coincided with the holidays or her children's birthdays, and it was then that I was especially aware of the poignancy of her caring for other kids as a profession. What I came to discover was that, as tough as those times were for her, they didn't dog her as I had thought, presumptively, they would. And I realized over time that I was imposing my own narrow view of the right and wrong ways to raise a family. Her kids finally did arrive a few years later to live with her, making for a happy ending. But luckily for us, it was happy all along.

THE SPECIALIST

We're expecting our first child soon and I'd love some help, but I don't feel ready to commit to hiring a full-time nanny yet. Is there any interim solution?

Baby nurses are quick-hit experts. They swoop to the rescue of frazzled new parents for a brief period—anywhere from five days to five weeks (although some parents rely upon them so much, they've been known to hold on to their baby nurses for months). Baby nurses camp out in the house and rarely complain about the accommodations (often just a sofa), or the grueling schedule of nonstop baby care. They're used to getting up several times a night to help with feedings and usually do the walking and rocking to sleep, post bottle or breast. True, you have no privacy for those days or weeks, but you're usually not concerned about that on two hours' sleep, anyway. And true, you'll most likely be subjected to a steady stream of opinions—which may come off as know-it-all. But we're talking a short time, and plenty of neophyte parents welcome the sure hand. Baby nurses, by the way, don't come cheap: Their rates can be as much as triple a regular nanny's weekly salary. A less expensive, less intrusive option for help during that initial getting-off-the-ground phase is a doula (Greek for female servant), a woman who comes in for a few hours a day to shop, cook, and clean a bit—to care for the mother as much as, or more, than for the baby. (Doulas are sometimes hired pre-delivery as well to help with everything from stocking the baby's room to practicing Kiegel exercises with the mother-to-be.) Parents who need less hand-holding through the diaper-bathe-burp-a-baby stage usually welcome this kind of maternally oriented help, because it pampers them and still leaves plenty of breathing room.

Overheard: The Godsend

When I was expecting my first child, my in-laws kept offering to hire a baby nurse for us as a gift. The whole notion bothered me. I wanted my husband and me to be alone with our newborn. The idea of a having a stranger in our small apartment, a person whose sole job was to feed and bathe our baby—the very things we'd been looking forward to doing for nine months—seemed odd and intrusive. So I politely declined. And I was glad we muddled through those sleepless nights without help; handling it all seemed a badge of honor. So I assumed I'd feel the same with my second child. Again, my in-laws offered, and again I declined. Then, that first night home, when our three-year-old daughter was still up at ten and the baby was wailing, I immediately thought better of it. This time, it wasn't the three of us getting to know each other—it felt more like two grumpy parents doing battle against two demanding children. I called my mother-in-law the next morning and that afternoon a charming woman named Sera arrived. By evening, the baby was happily napping in Sera's arms while she taught our three-year-old the names of Yankee infielders (it was World Series time), and my husband was walking around humming "Que Sera, Sera." She was only able to stay with us five days before she had to leave for another family (if only we'd reserved her ahead of time . . .). But by the time she went, we were hanging in there and felt that we could take over the helm.

Chapter 2

Where Do Nannies Come From?

Anytime parents get together and the conversation turns to childcare, the inevitable question arises, "How did you find your nanny?" For first-timers the whole hiring process can be as mystifying as a newborn itself. And for parents who already employ a caregiver, even one they adore, the search seems to be always ongoing. Situations change, needs change, people change—and the fact is, there is a lot of turnover in this business. While some families are fortunate enough to have the same nanny for ten years, most of us end up hiring a new caregiver every two or three. Or more. One couple played the nanny numbers game and figured out they'd had seventeen sitters in five years.

No matter how many times you've hired a sitter, you still have to begin each new search from ground zero. And no matter how jaded you are, you still think somewhere out there in the world there's a nanny who will answer all your needs, wants, and desires. But where to look? The place to start is simply with people you know. Work every social connection you can: cocktail parties, the office, book groups, the children's school. *Someone* always knows *someone* who knows *someone* who's in search of a job. Word of mouth, even at its most random or far-flung, usually delivers; it just may take a few days, weeks, or even months.

In the interest of time, and to hedge your bets, you may want to consider moving beyond your circle of friends and cast a wider net with a classified ad. A posting in a newspaper or on the Internet allows you to tap a large audience in one gesture. The trick is to weed out the possibles from the non-possibles without having to meet them all. You need to be specific in your wording: the number of days, your exact needs (someone who drives, likes animals, knows CPR), number of kids and ages, and whether English is a must. Even so, you'll need to go over the details again on the phone or via e-mail—you'd be surprised how many people answer ads even though they don't meet the criteria one bit.

Of course, the most direct way to find a sitter is at the source. Go where the nannies go—to bookstores, playgrounds, indoor play spaces—and do some on-the-spot recruiting. Caregivers are one of the best resources for other sitters—namely friends or relatives who are looking for work. You may even get lucky and meet a nanny who's soon to be in the market for a job herself, in which case you've just cut right to the interview stage.

If a hands-on search is getting you nowhere, or the whole endeavor is too exhausting to think about, you can always pay an agency to take over. These firms can speed up the process—need a nanny by Monday?—and save you a lot of legwork. The better agencies first interview the family, then suggest applicants that might be a good match (though, of course, they're also offering up those sitters they happen to have on deck). Often they ask the nannies to fill out a detailed application which they pass along to you, with questions like, "What would you do on a rainy day with a two-year-old?" and "What three nutritious meals could you prepare for a child's dinner?" Having this sketch ahead of time allows you to get more specific in your own questioning, and also gives you an idea of the nanny's ability to communicate—on paper, anyway.

Prescreening for potential liabilities is another perk offered by agencies who, theoretically, only register applicants who are qualified, legal and "clean." Many agencies also investigate criminal, driving, and child-abuse records—something most parents don't know how to do or don't bother to do on their own. And agencies all say they check references, but it's worth asking them to summarize those conversations and/or give you copies of their notes. As a cautionary tale, there's the story of the nanny who arrived in New York, fresh from England, and so charmed a couple of agencies with her British accent that they never bothered to verify her references—which may have been impeccable, but that's beside the point.

The most seductive aspect of agencies might be their role in brokering the deal: They typically negotiate the offer—salary, vacation, review. (They'll also break the bad news to rejected applicants.) For the person who doesn't like to get in the middle of all that sticky money stuff, the agency is a good bet. But it's not always a good deal. Most charge a flat fee of between one and two hundred dollars just to get into their system. Then, if you do end up hiring one of their caregivers, you're typically charged around 10 or 12 percent of her annual salary, anywhere from a thousand to twenty-five hundred dollars. Some people, however, think of it like a realtor's fee—it's tough to cough up the money, but once you've got the nanny, you want, what you had to do or pay to get there becomes irrelevant.

WORKING THE GRAPEVINE

I heard from my friend's sitter that her cousin's roommate is looking for work. Is this stretching word of mouth too far?

There's no such thing as too removed when you're trying to find a nanny. But the closer the tie, the better. More than three degrees of separation begins to get fuzzy. The whole point of working your connections is to hire someone through a mutual acquaintance, that way the sitter's reputation hinges on her doing a good job for you. Once you're considering a cousin's roommate, you're dealing with a total stranger. But that's not a reason to reject her out of hand. She may be terrific—or she may not be. You have to meet her and consider her with the same diligence you would any other candidate.

I've had a nanny "bequeathed" to me by a colleague who has been transferred out of town. The sitter seems great and comes highly recommended, but I've never hired a nanny before and have no frame of reference. Shouldn't I interview more people?

Don't look a gift horse in the mouth. You can't get much better than a personal reference, especially if you and your colleague are generally on the same wavelength. But don't be surprised if somewhere down the road, when the least bit of tension hits the air, you start wondering if you should have shopped around. The reality is that most parents go through this mental exercise: Even if you interviewed fifty people, you might speculate about the forty-nine you didn't choose. If you end up hiring "the gift" and you're happy with the relationship most of the time, spare yourself the woulda-coulda-shoulda angst.

Overheard: When Word of Mouth Boomerangs

About two years ago, I was desperate for a new live-in for our two kids, then five and eight, so I asked my friend's absolutely fantastic nanny if she had any friends who were looking for work. I was thrilled when she called that night with the number of a woman who she referred to as her "good buddy." The next day the prospective nanny called, and she sounded as charming as her friend. Her one ref-

erence checked out—and I assumed she was golden. But
from day one, it was clear she was not a happy camper.
She was glum, with a giant chip on her shoulder. She'd
look at the price tags of my daughter's clothes and mutter
something, and she'd do a half-hearted job of cleaning the
house. I should have let her go immediately, but I didn't
have a replacement lined up—and besides, I was in denial.
After two months, our caregiver's attitude seemed slightly
better and we offered her a bonus to stay with the children
while my husband and I went away to Santa Fe. On Monday, the day we were to depart, she didn't show up. I called
her at home, but there was no answer. Tuesday came, and
still no sign of her. The friend who had initially recommended her said she had no idea what had happened, and
in fact, they weren't really close friends at all—they'd just
met at a club a few months before. We ended up buying
two more plane tickets and our kids joined us for our ro-
mantic vacation. Two years later, we're still getting calls
from all kinds of creditors and loan officers in search of the
sitter. In retrospect I would have saved myself a lot of
trouble had I dug further and checked beyond her one glowing reference.

ADVERTISING YOURSELF

**My biggest fear about running an ad for a nanny in a newspaper
is exposing my phone number and address to all those strangers.**

True, unlike interviewing a new employee in an office situation,
you're opening up a very personal part of your life when you open
the door to your house. Unfortunately, loss of privacy is endemic
to the process. One way to get around putting your phone number
in the paper is to rent a voice mailbox from your local phone
company, which provides you with a separate and anonymous

answering service. And there's always the old post office box route if you've got the time to wait for written responses. But even if you do end up advertising with your home phone number, you can keep some distance by holding the initial meeting in neutral territory, like a coffee bar. If you get a good feeling about the candidate, go ahead and invite her for a home interview that day or the next. You can't—and shouldn't—avoid this second meeting at your house. She, too, needs to make an informed decision about where she's going to be spending much of her day-to-day life.

All my friends who have run ads for childcare tell me they've been overwhelmed by messages on the answering machine. I don't have the energy or time to meet twenty-five people, if that.

The only way to narrow the field is to be incredibly specific in the ad. If you want an experienced nanny, say so. If you want a woman, not a man, put that down (gender-discrimination rules do not apply to single-employee situations). If you want someone who drives, make that a requirement. It can take several tries before the first-time parent gets the wording of the ad just right. And no matter how precise, you still might be overwhelmed by responses. You can weed out about half on the basis of phone manner alone—too young/too ancient, too inarticulate/too chatty. Call back those candidates who sound promising and do another round of elimination; be explicit about schedule (they have to come at eight, stay until eight) and any special requirements you have (i.e., drive, swim, or cook). By engaging the candidates in conversation, you'll get a better sense of their communication skills—if you don't like what you hear on the phone, odds are you'll like it even less in person. In the end, you may only meet three or four candidates face to face, all of whom should be strong possibilities.

Nanny Point of view: Self-promotion

"I found that when I place my own ads under 'situations wanted,' I'm able to state who I am (mature, older woman), my limitations (I don't drive), the kind of kids I'm looking to care for (young), my flexibility (willing to work weekends), and what I think of as my strengths (love to cook, degree in art). By the time I go to meet the parents, I know I've already passed a few requirements."

I'm looking for a live-in and would love someone French speaking. Isn't it possible to go right to the source and hire someone from France who is willing to move here? Or is that a major hassle?

If you're willing to hire a young woman for only a year, the simplest route is to go through one of the six national au pair agencies (see appendix, p. 249). These are cultural exchange programs that place international au pairs with American host families (you can request a specific country of origin though you might not get it). But if you'd prefer someone a bit older or who can make more than a one-year commitment, advertising in a foreign-language newspaper—either in French or English or both—is the most feasible option. Start with the American editions of foreign papers—you may find a French native who is already living here. Next best, though a long-shot, is to advertise in a paper abroad.

To get a sense of an applicant half a world away, ask those who answer the ad to fill out an extensive written application and to send family photos, plus phone numbers for references. If you like what you see, set up a phone interview, and don't stint on the length of the conversation—it's too important. Once you find someone you'd want to hire, you then face the legal tangle of getting her a working visa. If you accomplish that, and she actually arrives, keep in mind that you'll have the responsibility of introducing her to a new culture (an advantage of the au pair agencies is that they create a network of support among the girls). Another thing to consider: The au pair needs a modicum of English to be able to communicate, not just with you, but with the world she's entered, especially if you will be leaving her on own and in charge.

With so many services proliferating on the Web, shouldn't I be able to find a nanny on-line?

As a go-between, the computer is fast and efficient but also limited to those nannies who go on line. The most inclusive way to search is to pursue all possible classified-type links. In this case, enter key words—nanny wanted, childcare help—and follow the leads. You'll bring up newspaper ads from all over the country, and of the hundreds of possible connections, many will be outdated, still leaving dozens of active sites for you to browse. You'll also come across many "advice-on-hiring" home pages that are really fronts for nanny agencies; they offer good basic info on salaries and such, but require a fee (a hundred dollars and up) for you to look at their listings. If you have a target group in mind—college students, vegetarians, or sitters with backgrounds in special needs—you can go directly to specific community bulletin boards on the Web. (Award for the most unusual posting: "Nudist/naturalist nanny wanted for two well-behaved children.") Most boards are public, meaning they allow you to be a voyeur of any job postings, not to mention post your own "help wanted" ad.

Overheard: College Recruiting

I called a nearby university with a good elementary-education program and told the career office I was looking for a part-time babysitter, about twenty hours per week.

She took all the info and sounded very encouraging. But then I got nothing—not one response the first or second week. So I called again. The placement officer said, "We have all your info right here in our book." And I thought, What college kid is going to go look in a book in the career office? So I made a bunch of flyers on the computer and pinned them around the campus—outside the eating hall, around common areas, on a few dorm bulletin boards. I got eight calls in one weekend, from college students and, in a few cases, their sisters or mothers. I ended up hiring a lively junior studying early childhood development who said she and her friends always scan the flyers for jobs.

COVETING THY NEIGHBOR'S NANNY

The woman in the apartment below me has a wonderful, warm nanny taking care of her children. I had my first baby a few months ago and haven't been able to find someone who seems half as good. I'm debating whether to approach the nanny and ask if she's happy with her job.

You're probably so infatuated with this nanny that you're not thinking about how awkward it would be every time you and the neighbor rode the elevator together. (And, anyway, who knows if the everyday reality of this nanny would measure up?) Instead of approaching the sitter, approach the employers and see if they'd mind asking their caregiver for names of friends or relatives looking for work. You never know: Your neighbors may be thinking of making a change in their own childcare situation, making their sitter fair game. At least you've left the door open. What you don't want to do is go behind someone's back—bad form in any business.

Our sitter needed to go away for a few weeks and sent her friend over as a replacement. We all fell in love with the friend. She's funny, charming, and upbeat, in contrast to our regular sitter who tends to be a bit sullen. We know the girlfriend is unemployed and are tempted to ask her to work for us.

Put yourself in your sitter's shoes. How would you like to be betrayed by your boss *and* by your friend? And if your nanny is trustworthy and good with the children, are you sure you'd want to trade her for a little-known entity? The real issue is, just how unhappy *are* you with the current nanny—or how unhappy is she? Your energy may be better spent figuring out the answers to these questions.

Overheard: The Two-Timing Nanny

When a new family moved in across the street, our long-time sitter suddenly found every reason to be over there. Maybe it's because they have a brand new kitchen and a big backyard. Maybe it's because their kids are older than ours, and not so demanding. Whatever, she began offering to babysit for them at night and started turning up there on the weekends. Finally, our neighbor called me sheepishly and explained that our caregiver had offered to work for her full time. She was feeling me out. I said, "No way, I need her." After my initial hurt, I asked our nanny why she wanted to leave. She was embarrassed at the way I'd found out about it, but she eventually opened up. She felt completely overworked and burned out. We made a deal that she could leave a little earlier in the evening when the kids tend to be really wild, and I'd take back the grocery shopping duty. She was clearly relieved, and happily for us, began to refocus on our family, where her attention belonged.

PICK-UP LINES

I take my three-year-old to a music class at the local Y, and have become friendly with a young woman who brings her charge, a three-year-old girl. The nanny came up to me the other day and told me she's been looking for another job. It just so happens I need someone, but this doesn't feel quite right.

In the corporate world, people jump ship all the time—for more money, better benefits, nicer working conditions. If she's unhappy, and you don't know her boss, you're free to poach. But when checking her references, make a point of asking her former employers how long she was on the job and why she left. What you're looking for is any pattern of chronic dissatisfaction, as in the nanny who switches venues the second she's bored. If she passes muster, encourage her to give her employer ample notice—you'd want the same.

Since my sitter left, I've been spending a lot of time at the neighborhood playground with my toddler. I've had the chance to observe a group of caregivers day in and out, and one woman in particular has caught my eye. I'm thinking of approaching her about a job.

There's nothing better than seeing a nanny in action, especially when she's not performing for her employer. And there's no law against striking up a conversation. If you like her, let her know that if she finds herself out of a job anytime in the near future, she can call you. In the meantime, ask if she has any friends looking for work as caregivers—and, if so, could she bring them along to the park? This provides the perfect no-pressure way to meet and "interview" a prospective nanny en plein air.

Overheard: Looking in All the "Wrong" Places

The two best nannies I ever employed weren't even nannies when I hired them. I met the first on a Saturday when I went shopping in a department store for something to wear to an upcoming party. I had my three-month-old-daughter with me, and the young woman who was helping me kept oohing and aahing over the baby. She asked me if I'd like her to hold the baby while I tried on the umpteenth black dress she'd found for me, and said, "Don't worry, I babysit a lot during the week." She seemed very natural with the baby and enchanted by her. After she rang up the dress I bought, she asked me if I needed someone to watch my daughter. In fact, I'd just started to look, so I took her number and the names of some references. She ended up working for us weekdays, while keeping her weekend sales job.

Our next sitter happened to be the cashier at our favorite coffee shop. We'd see her every morning when we stopped by for breakfast, and became quite friendly with her. One day, when we were paying the check, we asked her if she had any friends who might be interested in babysitting. She surprised us by saying, "Actually, I'm interested." We knew she was reliable (she was there every day), and that she did did the restaurant's books, which in our minds meant the owner trusted her. She also said she used to work with kids and wanted to again, adding that she could use a little more income—it turned out she was only making minimum wage. We took her on, and she stayed with us through the birth of our second child. A lot of my friends who've found their nannies through agencies or ads were skeptical of our unconventional search approach. But clearly, for us it's worked.

THE AGENCY AVENUE

I was all set to sign on with a local nanny agency, until I got a load of their fees. What can an agency do that could possibly be worth $1,500?

In return for their high fees, agencies offer a kind of do-it-all deal: They take a lot of the think-work and anxiety out of the whole hiring process by suggesting starting salaries and vacation policies. They may even set you up with ancillary services, like accountants to handle nanny-tax issues or payroll departments to issue weekly checks. Another benefit is that they conduct basic research on the applicants, including criminal checks, plus they're experienced interviewers who are likely to pick up inconsistencies between a nanny's resume and her references. Some agencies go so far as to intervene or mediate if you have trouble down the road. But, perks aside, an agency is only as strong as its current pool of applicants— no single firm has a lock on extraordinary nannies.

I'm paying off the books—are agencies out of the question?

Surprisingly, many agencies leave parents and nannies to work out the question of paying legally. And although there's a paper trail—the agency has a record of when the employee started and how much she's making—the IRS has not made a habit of subpoenaing agency files. Not yet, anyway.

There are five agencies in my area—is there any reason I can't register with all five at once?

Basic registration fees range from one hundred to two hundred and fifty dollars, so you could be spending close to a thousand to hook up with all five. (And remember, you'll also pay a hefty fee to the agency you hire through). By signing up with everyone in town, however, you'll get a bigger field of candidates to meet, although since nannies can register with multiple agencies, you may also get some overlap of candidates. As far as agencies are concerned, like real estate agents, they prefer exclusivity but can't legally demand it.

Nanny Point of View: The Ups and Downs of Agencies

"The major advantage to using an agency is that you don't have to be very aggressive in your search. But there are many cons, too. Agencies are often concerned about placing you as quickly as possible without much regard to whether it's the best match. And sometimes, families who hire through an agency pay a little less in salary to compensate for the high placement fees—so the idea that you're paid more through an agency is often just a myth."

What if I decide I'm not happy with the nanny's performance after I've hired her through an agency? Am I obligated to keep her or can I request a replacement? A refund?

Most agencies offer a trial period—two or three months is the most common, although sometimes you'll get a year or longer— in which they'll send you new candidates without charging you more money. But keep in mind, you may not get the top banana; agencies tend to reserve their strongest candidates for those incoming clients who will be paying them a fat new fee. (And anyway, don't be too quick to bail. The two-month trial is not totally arbitrary; that's about how long it takes for some nannies, and some families, to adjust to one another.) As for refunds, it's a rare agency that will give you your money back, although some will return a percentage of the fee within the trial period if you don't like any the proposed replacements. Odds are, when you signed on, you gave up any rights to hold the agency responsible for a nanny's behavior. Even in extreme cases—say, the nanny cleaned out your bank account, stole your car, and left your kids home alone—your problem lies with her, not with the agency.

A Quick Study: Is She Legal?

Where nannies come from—literally—becomes a very relevant question if the caregiver you've set your sights on is not a U.S. citizen. Immigration matters are immensely complicated, and many parents would rather remain ignorant of them than take the time to figure them out, on the wishful theory that if they don't know the law, they're not breaking the law. For those want to be debriefed, here's a primer on the immigration terms you're most likely to encounter, and what they mean vis-à-vis your, and her, legal position and liability.

Sponsorship is a process through which employers fill out paperwork (a lot of it) on behalf of someone who's foreign-born, requesting a green card for them (*see below*) so that they may work and live in this country legally. Most parents hire an immigration attorney who knows the ins and outs of immigration law, which has changed in the last few years. Generally, sponsorship takes anywhere from one to three years; during that period you vouch that the sponsoree won't be a burden to society (i.e., get in trouble with the law or go on welfare). Up to three years is a long time to be responsible for someone who is not a relative, which is why so few parents embark on the process. And, by the way, if you hire someone illegally with the *intent* to sponsor her, you are still, technically, breaking the law.

Green card is a document that is actually green. Someone who holds one of these coveted cards has been sponsored for immigration and can legally work and live in the United States in the interim. It's harder for nannies to get green cards now than it was a few years ago since immigration is more difficult in general. In addition, because nannies are considered "unskilled" workers, it's difficult to prove that there is no one in the United States equally qualified to do the work.

Permanent residents are one step from becoming citizens. The green-card–carrying caregiver is free to stay in the United States, although she has to reapply for her permanent residency every three years and she can't vote. After five years, permanent residents can apply for naturalization (to become U.S. citizens)— and at that point they give up citizenship of their home country. In terms of employment, it's legal to hire a resident anywhere along the process, from the first day she gets her residency to the time she becomes a citizen.

Illegal alien is really two terms in one. "Illegal," in this case, refers to someone who has skirted the immigration law by entering the United States without the proper visa or paperwork; and "alien" refers to anyone who is not a U.S. citizen. Obviously, hiring an illegal alien is—no bones about it—illegal.

Political or religious asylum is a low-odds ways for nannies (or anyone, for that matter) to enter the country. The person seeking asylum has to demonstrate a well-founded fear of persecution in her homeland—which is difficult to prove. And even if she were to qualify, there's no guarantee she'd get a green card at the end of the process. The political or religious climate in her country may have changed for the better, leaving her without a strong case and with the strong possibility of being deported.

Chapter 3

The Art of the Interview

You sit down across from a stranger who's interested in taking care of your child. You ask a few questions, jot down a few notes, and then talk money. You don't know this person, yet you're about ready to hire her. It's odd, and interesting, how cavalier we can be when it comes to choosing a nanny, often taking less time than we would in picking other kinds of professionals in our lives, whether it's an office assistant or an interior designer. The reason is probably twofold. Many of us feel awkward hiring domestic help, especially if we didn't grow up with any. And in our desire to find someone we like and tie up the loose ends—so we can get back to work, get on with our lives—we're eager to hire the first appealing candidate. During the interview, we're willing to gloss over the hard-to-ask questions; we don't want to intrude too much so we step lightly when it comes to personal or delicate subjects. Quite often, too, there's an underlying wish on the parents' part to be liked, to be "picked" by the nanny. So we present ourselves as easygoing, not too nosy, not too pushy—the soft sell.

Of course, some people go the other route. They grill each prospective candidate with a prescribed list of questions, and are determined to stick by a preconceived idea of "perfect." These parents may suffer from not being able to see the forest through the trees—they're wedded to the image of a young, energetic go-getter, when what's staring them in the face is an older, loving, maternal woman who just could be that perfect nanny. The over-zealous interviewer is on a quest for the best: the most experi-enced, the most confident, the most athletic. And, of course, the smartest. But it's easy to overvalue intelligence (how many times have we heard, "she's too bright to be doing this, we're lucky to have her"); education is no predictor of a loving or even com-petent professional. Don't discount other qualities that are equally, if not more key than book smarts: warmth, cuddliness, calmness, agreeability, sense of humor, sparkle.

So, what are you actually going to talk about during this con-versation? Start with the obvious: the schedule of hours and a detailed description of the job. Many parents report that, in ret-rospect, they wish they had been more explicit about what they wanted in terms of light household chores and what they didn't want in terms of visitors, say, or phone calls. It's much easier to lay out all the rules and responsibilities up front than to back into them later. If, after you've stated the terms, the nanny still seems interested, move on to talk about her: where she's from, where she's worked. Then throw in a few open-ended questions, which will give you a window into the candidate's character. One parent we know of asked, "What in your life has prepared you for this kind of job?" The nanny answered, "I come from a divorced household and I realize how important security is in a child's life, so I want to be a strong, reliable friend." Another parent asked, "Aside from childcare, what have you accomplished that you're proud of?" And the nanny answered, "I was happy when I brought a neglected and skittish horse along to be a kind pleasure horse." Both these responses revealed a caring nature, an empathetic at-titude. The kind of pat question that *doesn't* offer much insight is, "What do you like most about being a nanny?" The applicant knows the "right" answer is simply to say, "I love kids."

To ask the questions you need to ask, and get the answers you need to hear, don't rush the meeting. An average interview lasts thirty minutes or so, but if you're seriously considering the candidate, an hour is not too long. (If you're sure she's a no-go from the start, ten minutes is polite.) Don't worry if you forget to ask a certain question; you can always call back—a good idea in any case: How a sitter responds, and sounds, on the phone may give you strong clues about the way the two of you will be communicating every day, especially if you work outside the home. Articulate, expansive answers are clearly more inspiring than mumbling, vague responses or a string of yesses and noes.

Basically, you've got two things to take away from an interview: first impressions and references. What to make of your intuitive reactions? In this case, a lot. You know right away if you like someone—the way she comports herself, acts, talks. You know what makes you uncomfortable. Don't ignore your private prejudices—against too much makeup, or too few teeth. As much as you may hate to admit to them, they're not likely to go away overnight. At the same time, you also have to cut a prospective sitter a little slack. Anyone who's been on an interview knows that nerves can undercut confidence, making one appear less capable than one really is.

As for references, request them—and check them. In an effort to land a first job, applicants occasionally fake a reference (using a bogus name or that of a relative), hoping you won't follow up. Even if a person comes recommended by a good friend—best-case scenario—you absolutely must call. In this round of interrogation, start with the broad-stroke questions, such as, "What was she like with the children?" or "would you hire her again?" Then zero in on specifics: "If you had to name three negative qualities about so and so, what would it be?" This kind of deliberate questioning forces the other parent off automatic pilot, jarring his or her memory a bit to reveal characteristics that aren't so obvious. These added insights, along with your own instincts, make for a more complete and realistic portrait.

FIRST IMPRESSIONS

**We've just interviewed a nanny who came with glowing rec-
ommendations from several families we know rather well. So
we expected someone outgoing and confident, but she seems a
bit quiet, even withdrawn. Could all her references be off?**

Chances are she takes time to warm up—many people are shy on
interviews, then become outgoing and self-assured in the day-to-
day rhythm of the job. Check back with the other families to see
if they remember her being reserved at the beginning. There's
also the possibility that her reticence is due to her lack of enthusiasm with the outline of the job. Maybe it's the money, maybe
the hours, maybe the household responsibilities. In any case, if
you laid out the job without giving her a chance to respond or
interrupt, you won't know which of the issues, if any, rubbed her
the wrong way. On a follow-up phone call, you could go over the
description of the job again in detail, and at each point, ask how
it sits with her. The last thing you want is to have her accept the
job reluctantly. You'll just find yourself having to win over a disgruntled employee—no fun for anyone.

**The first nanny we met we immediately adored but she said she
needs to start right away. I don't want to make a rash decision
but I don't want to lose her to another family by waiting.**

Even if a prospective sitter tells you she's got another offer, resist
the temptation to hire under pressure—you're probably not going
to lose anyone overnight or in a day. It's always a good idea to
let impressions percolate. After sleeping on it, you might remember that you forgot to ask a few key things, such as whether she
smokes (you're terribly allergic) or whether she has her green card

(you've decided you only want to hire legally). If the good impression holds, and all the questions are answered take the leap; instincts are one of the best gauges we have in this arena.

A sweet, well-mannered woman interviewed with us, and in my mind I'd decided she was it. As I walked her to the door, I told her I'd let her know soon, and she answered, "It will be Jesus' wish." I have nothing against religion per se, but extremes of any kind make me nervous.

What most parents *don't* want in a nanny is someone who brings to the table a strong agenda of any kind—religious, political, ideological—that has nothing to do with childcare. Understandably, parents want to control the kinds of attitudes and influences that pervade the household, and so if anything strikes a discordant note in the first meeting, don't ignore it. Follow your private peeves, even if they're politically incorrect.

Nanny Point of View: The Rote Approach

"I went on an interview the other day that was fine on the surface, but I left feeling they couldn't possibly have known who I really was. The questions they asked were resume-type questions—where I grew up, where I went to school, how long I'd been a caregiver—but nothing about the kinds of projects I like to do with kids or the way I'd spend an afternoon, or even the ages of children I'd worked with. All they were concerned with was the schedule and the money. I found myself answering in one- or two-word sentences, and we never got any real conversation rolling."

Overheard: Staying Open-Minded

A year ago we moved with a newborn and a two-year-old out of the city to a small town and advertised in the local paper for a nanny. Of those who responded, I liked one immediately: She was a middle-aged woman, a mother of four. It turned out, however, that she didn't have a driver's license, and I'd decided I really needed someone who drove. She said she understood, but before she left she asked to hold the baby. She seemed really comfortable and happy with our son in her arms. I went on to interview others, but she stuck in my mind. After a few weeks, when I hadn't found anyone I was crazy about, I called her to ask if she would work for me on a temporary basis. She was very agreeable, never pressed to know more about my search, and I realized how at ease I was with her. I ultimately decided the driving wasn't as important as I'd thought. She's been with us for a year now, and while I sometimes find it inconvenient to chauffeur the kids around, I realize it's not as big a deal as I thought it would be, and certainly her inability to drive is less critical than her ability to nurture.

PRICKLY QUESTIONS

I feel funny about asking sensitive questions, such as "Have you ever been arrested or had a drinking problem?" But I do want to know. Is there a subtle way to ask or to find out?

One way to avoid the awkwardness is to give candidates a simple questionnaire with space for all the pertinent name/age/phone number info, as well as a few "big" questions, like those concerning criminal records or any alcohol or drug problems. While there's no harm in asking, you can't guarantee an honest answer (which is probably why many parents don't bother). You can also, of course, ask in person—the advantage being that you'll have a chance to read the applicant's body language; any hesitation or averted eye contact could be red flag. Another tactic is to go straight to the references. Grill them with pointed questions such as, "Did you ever suspect of her of drinking on the job?" "Did you ever see signs of drug abuse? Or an eating disorder?" "Was she ever involved in any legal or financial trouble?" "Did she ever show erratic behavior or have wild mood swings?" You might feel awkward asking, but if there were any problems, you'd rather know than not.

I've heard it's illegal to ask someone's age, sexual orientation, and whether they've had a recent AIDS test. These happen to be things I'm concerned about, but I don't want to overstep any boundaries.

While it may feel incredibly nosy, even morally repugnant, it's not illegal to ask a nanny applicant anything you want: whether she's ever been sexually or physically abused, whether she's taking any psychiatric medication, as well as questions about age and marital status—present and past. Companies with larger numbers of employees, and more occasions for promotions and raises, are not allowed to discriminate based on any of these factors. But the law says if you're employing fewer than fifteen people, you can ask anyone any question, with the possible exception (in some states) of whether they are gay or straight or bi.

My previous nanny, it turned out, had a phobia about snakes and would never kneel down in the yard with our two-year-old,

**which really bugged me. How can I be sure there'll be no sur-
prises this time?**

While it's hard to ferret out every fear and phobia, major ones
should certainly be brought up: swimming, driving, flying,
heights, darkness, storms, and being alone in the night. Some will
be germane, others not. Maybe she can't be in the same room
with a dog, which is okay if you plan never to own one. But let's
say you're a family who travels a lot, and want to take the sitter
along—fear of flying would be a big problem. To try to pinpoint
potential fears that can trip up a normal day, go through your
child's routine and ask the nanny if any specific thing bothers
her: taking the kids to school (up an elevator?); to an indoor pool
(germ paranoia?); to soccer practice (over the bridge?). If you can
both navigate the day without a hitch, you've eliminated most
surprises.

**A nanny we're considering has been very open about her epi-
lepsy. She says the condition is under complete control with
medication and she hasn't had a seizure in five years. I don't
want to be close-minded, but it makes me nervous to hire someone with a medical problem.**

You need to educate yourself so you know if your concern is based
on fact or fear. In the case of epilepsy—or diabetes or asthma,
for instance—it's possible to keep the condition under control
with medication. Ask for the nanny's permission to speak with
her doctor to make sure there are no issues about driving the kids,
spending the night, or needing time off for frequent doctor's visits. And ask the physician whether she's responsible when it
comes to managing her health—a good sign she's responsible in
other arenas as well.

INTERVIEWING EN FAMILLE

Shouldn't I have the kids around to meet the prospective nannies? After all, the relationship is really between them.

Yes and no. The relationship between the adults is equally important, if not more so. Most kids adapt to anyone with a basic level of competence and warmth—grown-ups are tougher to throw together and tougher to please. And although by having the kids on hand you do get some sense of how natural the caregiver is with children, the situation is hardly a natural one. You may find yourself jumping up to get juice for a toddler or shooing away a nine-year-old who is trying to perform a piano piece for the newcomer—and may end the interview without getting basic information about the prospective nanny. If time is not an issue for either of you, however, observing that interaction certainly can't hurt.

THE UNREVEALING CONVERSATION

After an interview has ended, I find I don't know or can't remember very much about the nanny even though I've spent almost an hour talking with her.

Maybe you did all the talking. Many of us spend so much time describing the job, we don't ask enough questions—or we ask the kinds of questions that elicit yes/no responses. Anyway, you won't retain as much as you think, especially if you interview several candidates in a row. To get yourself in a more journalistic frame of mind, take notes both about the facts and your impressions (open smile, relaxed or a bit uptight, no eye contact). If you feel scattered, and aren't having much luck keeping all the interviewees straight in your head—or you tend to scribble on little bits of paper that you later lose—you might want to formalize the process with an application she can fill out on the spot; this will give you a record of names, numbers, and past employers—the kinds of details you might easily forget to take down in the middle of a good conversation.

CHOOSING BETWEEN A FEW GOOD WOMEN

I interviewed five employees and all five are fine, but no one stands out. I need to hire someone soon. How do I decide?

A lot of parents find it helpful to hire a few candidates on a day basis—you'll get a feel for their styles, and you'll get the child-care you need. You'd be surprised by how much you can learn about a person in a day. And the kids, if they're at the verbal stage, can give you their input. A word of advice: Don't make the common mistake of putting the house in order, literally and figuratively, before she comes. The more chaotic and true-to-life the scenario, the better a feel you'll have for her ability to jump in and take charge. If you're waffling between two prospects, have them come by on consecutive days so your comparisons are fresh—and have them do similar tasks: Ask them both to do an art project with the kids and to straighten up the kitchen, for instance. One might make papier-maché masks and scrub the counters; the other may make a half-hearted attempt at coloring and just stack the dirty dishes in the sink. After that, it's unlikely you'll feel exactly the same way about both.

Nanny Point of View: What Swayed Me

"I was trying to decide between two job offers. Both interviews went really well, but there was something about one of the families, actually the one that was offering more money, that didn't sit well with me. The house was so perfect, everything in its place; the children were wearing head-to-toe coordinated outfits;

and, what made me hesitate most of all, was the way the parents spoke to me—in a very formal, slightly condescending manner. I just couldn't imagine myself feeling at home in their house. I went with the family who was a little sloppier, had two more kids and longer hours, but seemed a lot more easygoing."

READING (INTO) A REFERENCE

When we called the former employers of the nanny we want to hire, all three said she was just "okay." How much stock do you put in the opinions of people you've never met?

It's always hard to be in the middle of other people's relationships, but you've got to go with the references you have unless it's clear from the conversation that your take on things is radically different from theirs—she likes everything in place, in order, on time, and you're much looser. It's also possible that your circumstances aren't anything like those of the former employers—and that the nanny could be great for you even if the situation didn't work out for them. Maybe the sitter isn't flexible about hours and can't stay late, but you work at home and, for you, this wouldn't be an issue. Or maybe she's an introvert, but that's not the kind of thing that bothers you. Still, if you're getting a lot of polite but lukewarm feedback, don't ignore it.

The former boss of a nanny we're considering was very polite when I asked reference questions. But he wasn't very forthcoming—I wasn't able to get very much out of him.

Most people don't want to ruin someone's chances for a job, especially if they feel responsible in any way for the demise of a relationship. You'll need to prod a bit more. This is a case where ten very pointed yes/no questions are actually better than a few soft questions. Get specific—not, "Was she good with the kids?" but, "Did she sit on the floor and read to them?" Make a list of what really matters to you—getting the kids outside every day, taking decent phone messages, keeping the house in order, promptness—and you'll get a much better idea of how well suited she is to the job.

We're thinking of hiring a sitter who has never been a nanny before. How do we check her references if she hasn't any?

She does, just not the kind you're thinking of. If she's had any job experience, you can get a lot out of her former employers— was she responsible, punctual, easy to work with, well liked? For clues to personality you can also tap teachers and neighbors. Ask not only about her general temperament and job performance, but specifically whether they've observed her caring for children. You want to make sure a novice has plenty of personal experience with kids or, if relevant, with infants. And if all her former references have mysteriously "moved," leaving no forwarding number, you'd best pass on her no matter how great she seems.

A QUICK STUDY: THE BACKGROUND CHECK

The truth is, the majority of employers don't bother to do criminal background checks—they may feel uncomfortable poking around someone's private life, or assume the best of people, or think that the investigations are complicated and expensive. But as many as one in twenty nanny checks come up with something you'd want to know about—maybe not the big stuff, but petty crimes like shoplifting or passing bad checks. If you're tempted to investigate (because you're cautious by nature or you've been burned before), tracking down a PI is no big deal. If you can't find one through word of mouth or through a nanny agency that you're signed on with, simply check the yellow pages (under Investigators—private), which has no shortage of ads—look for those that list background checks as part of their service. Don't agonize too much over who to choose since even the tiniest firms can handle this most basic investigation, which typically runs $50–100 and takes two to five days to complete. (If your check covers multiple states the fee could double or triple.) It's up to you whether you want to come clean to the nanny about the fact you're checking her out (you're not required by law to tell her or get her consent). But it may be to your advantage to be up front about the investigation. That way, you don't have to make excuses or stall about why you're waiting to hire her; some parents even make the hire contingent upon the results of the search. Anyway, if the prospective nanny gets a little too antsy at the whole idea, or says she can't wait a few days, that's a red flag in and of itself. Here's what a routine check covers:

Criminal Since only the FBI has access to a national criminal database, the best an investigator can do is check crime records for every state the nanny's lived in (the ones you know of). Some states—namely Colorado, Connecticut, Florida, Georgia, Hawaii, Missouri, Montana, North Dakota, Oklahoma, Oregon, South Carolina, and Washington, as well as the District of Columbia—have databases that are extremely easy to check; in the rest of the country red tape mires the process, so it's probably more efficient and effective to ask for a county-by-county check.

Credit While you probably don't give a hoot if she once bounced a check, you should pay attention if she's repeatedly behind on her credit cards or has ever been in default of her loan—tips offs to irresponsibility. But if you really like the sitter give her a chance to explain: A lousy record may just be ancient history that's since been rectified (credit checks go back seven years).

Driving Again, you're not looking for a single speeding ticket but a pattern of recklessness. And certainly any DWI is cause for pause.

Social Security Number Verification This tells you two things: one, that she's legal (She doesn't have to be a U.S. citizen to have a social security number—resident aliens, who are from another country but in the United States legally have social security cards as well); and two, that what she says about basic facts— name, age—check out.

Part II

The Pay Package

Chapter 4

Setting the Salary

Money—no surprise—stirs up more conflicts, insecurities, and agita between nanny and parent than almost any other topic. Talking salary—starting pay, overtime, makeup hours—can cause the most voluble sorts to clam up or the most reserved to babble incoherently. Even if the conversation ends up being one-sided, there are two parties to please. And in this business, there's often a dichotomy at the core: Parents talk about being tapped out by the cost of childcare; nannies say they feel underpaid. At the most basic level, you're the boss, so you decide what you want to offer; she's the employee, she decides what she needs to make, and hopefully you're somewhere in the same ballpark.

When it comes to throwing out a number, it helps to have parameters to work within. The only industry standard is that created by your peers, in your region. Salaries tend be highest on the East Coast with Manhattan and its wealthier suburbs commanding mind-boggling rates. In California and Florida, nanny wages tend to be slightly lower, in part because there's so much illegal immigrant labor to draw from. On average, however, common starting salaries run somewhere around $400 per week for 40 to 50 hours, with $275 or $800 not unheard of at either extreme. Higher-end wages usually take into account one or more of these factors: the days are longer than ten hours; the nanny is experienced (over five years), college-educated, and can drive; there are more than two children; or there's quite a bit of housework involved. Nannies who get top dollar are often more than nannies—some are like household managers: they may shop, cook, clean, order flowers, iron sheets, buy the kids' clothes, and keep track of staples from paper towels to mineral water.

Once a number is set, a salary typically remains the same week to week, even if the hours vary slightly in either direction—say, you send the sitter home an hour early or you come home half an hour late. Everyone's circumstances and pay thresholds are different, but there's one accepted precept: In figuring out a wage, don't be too cheap. Babysitters talk, they network, they compare notes. And be savvy: If you hire a friend of one of your friends' nannies, try to pay on a par, or you risk at least one disgruntled employee.

In the case of part-time or sporadic babysitting, paying by the hour is more practical. Hourly wages in most of the country range from seven to fifteen dollars, with ten dollars the norm. There's also the option of paying an hourly wage to full-time nannies rather than a salary: Some parent work schedules (irregular) and some parent styles (to-the-letter types) are better suited to this arrangement. Because the hours are tallied daily or weekly, there's no shelling out for unused time. Employers who use the hourly system often promise a minimum weekly figure so the nanny's take-home pay isn't left to the whims of the week. But if you clock a lot of hours, you could end up paying a higher weekly wage. At twelve dollars an hour, a forty-eight-hour week nets $576, up to one hundred and fifty dollars more than for a salaried wage.

Now to the truly tricky question: On or off the books? Paying cash is illegal, of course, but oh-so simple—not a jot of paperwork. And many nannies prefer it; they take home more cash, and don't pay any taxes. But there's a risk in flouting the law. One day an ex-babysitter may try to collect unemployment and—

wait—the employer never filed unemployment taxes. Not only is the nanny without recourse, the employer's busted and will have to pay back taxes plus fines. If you haven't paid it, she's not eligible, and you're exposed.

There's also a kind of subtle collusion that goes on when you pay under the table, which may feel cozy but can backfire: In the crudest terms, your employee has something on you. While a nanny may be like family now, you don't know how she'll feel once the relationship is over. Paying the tax is definitely a bit of a hassle, but the repercussions of *not* paying could prove to be even more of one.

How Much Is Enough?

The caregiver we have for our one-year-old son is close to ideal. I have no complaints, just guilt: After talking to friends, I realize I'm paying far less than they are for the same number of hours. Our caregiver doesn't seem unhappy and I can't really afford more—but I don't want to be a cheapskate.

As they say, there's more to a job than money. If you think your sitter is happy, then she probably is—don't look for a problem. Let's assume that your child is easygoing, that you are relaxed, even-tempered employers, and that the environment is a pleasant one; these intangibles are worth a lot. Compare that to making fifty dollars more a week working for a tyrannical boss, with hysterical children, in a house full of don't-touch-this, don't-eat-that rules. We know of more sitters who have quit under those circumstances than the other scenario. You can always give a perk, in the form of an afternoon off now and then.

We planned on paying $375 a week for childcare, but the nanny we'd love to hire originally said she needed substantially more.

Even so, she seems to really want the job, but I worry that she'll always be looking for something higher paying.

A nanny who takes less money than she says she wants is likely to consider the job a stopgap—and leave for a better offer in a heartbeat. And even while she stays, you may face tension with her over things involving money. You might feel uncomfortable, for example, about splurging on anything in her presence and she may reproach you, silently or otherwise. A little salary negotiation is called for. If your initial figure and hers are within a hundred dollars of each other, try to raise yours by half the difference and you'll start off on a better footing.

Nanny Point of View: The "Con" of Paying off the Books

"In my experience, if a family wants to 'cheat' by not paying a nanny on the books, they will probably cheat the nanny somewhere else along the way. The desire to pay under the table shows a lack of respect for the profession and it raises the question of whether the family can afford to hire a nanny in the first place."

We recently moved from a major urban area to a smaller city—shouldn't the prices for babysitting services be dramatically lower?

It's one of the ironies of the market that prices in smallish cities (think Portland, Maine; Dayton, Ohio; Nashville, Tennessee) are as high or higher than in notoriously expensive cities like Manhattan. There's a smaller pool of potential applicants to draw on (not to mention a smaller immigrant population), which means there's more competition among parents for qualified nannies.

Likewise, suburban salaries tend to be on par with urban wages— even when they're slightly lower, you may end up paying the nanny's commuting costs, which brings the pay right back up in the same league.

Overheard: The Strategy of Starting Low

We'd always paid a competitive salary for experienced nannies, but after a while we felt we wasted an awful lot of money on people who didn't work out. (Once we had four nannies in one year.) So my husband and I tried a new approach. Rather than offering top dollar to attract so-called top talent, we dropped the salary by $100 or so and looked for less experienced, young women for whom we provided a first real nanny job. To make up for the low starting salary, we promised to give a $25 raise after three months, another raise after six, a third after nine months, and a fourth after she'd been with us an entire year. From the sitter's point of view, if she stuck with us, she'd be guaranteed a decent and generous salary in a short period of time. From our point of view it took away the distrust. And it worked.

HOW MUCH IS TOO MUCH?

We've typically paid our part-time sitters $10 an hour. Now I'm returning to work full time and I'm trying to calculate a salary; ten dollars multiplied by a fifty-hour work week sounds awfully high for starting pay.

While ten dollars an hour is not unusual for "freelance" babysitting (the range is anywhere from seven to fifteen), weekly salaries are usually based on a lower hourly rate—the logic being that salaried positions have other things going for them, namely, the security of a steady income and paid vacation time. Try multiplying your hours by eight or nine dollars, even seven if she's not that experienced, and you'll come up with a number that's more doable and still competitive.

The person I want to hire seems perfect, but she's asking us to match the high salary she was making with her previous family. Am I expected to do that, or is it reasonable to ask her to start at a lower rate and work her way up?

Yes and no. You certainly can't start where she started out. Not only has the nanny accumulated all those years of experience, the market has gone up considerably (if her beginning pay was $275 ten years ago, that's more like $375 in today's dollars). And you may not know the whole story behind the salary—maybe the nanny worked very long hours, maybe the parents traveled frequently, maybe she had a heavy housework load. Keep in mind, also, that her salary reflects consistent annual raises. In any case, you need to arrive at a figure—a compromise of $425, say—that makes her feel like she's not stepping down and gives you room to raise her pay over time.

I interviewed a terrific woman who says she'll not only take care of our two kids, but also cook for the family, clean the whole house, and do all the laundry. The rub is she wants one-third more than we had budgeted for the job.

A cook-housekeeper-nanny in one is a pretty appealing package. If she really can pull off all these household chores and give the kids plenty of attention, then it might be a reasonable deal. In terms of justifying the cost, look at it this way: If you currently have a cleaning lady come in you could eliminate that cost, lowering the nanny's salary, for all intents and purposes. And a nanny who cooks, freeing you from kitchen duty, and who takes the entire laundry load off you may be invaluable—that, you have to decide.

The Deal with Part-Timers

A friend is scaling back the hours of her full-time sitter to two days a week. I'm interested in picking up her other three days. How do you pay a shared nanny?

It's a bit complicated to share a salary—your hours, vacations, holiday schedules will likely be different from your friend's. Better to cut your own separate deal and give your own separate salary. In this situation, some parents prefer to pay by the day—typically seventy-five to a hundred dollars for eight to ten hours—because they want the flexibility to add or subtract days from week to week—three days one week, two days the next—assuming the partner-in-employment is also flexible. If, however, neither of you needs the sitter on a particular day, you're still on the hook; it goes without saying that the sitter was promised five days, and she should be paid for all of them.

Our son is in day care, but we're looking to hire someone for a few hours in the evening to pick him up, bring him home, and make him dinner. I've heard you have to pay a premium for part-time help.

In one of those logical/illogical quirks of the market, it's true that the fewer the hours you employ someone, the more you may need to pay per hour. Work paid by the hour usually runs one or two dollars per hour more than salaried work. This is why some parents put together package deals: A set amount for the week—say $125—covering one-and-a-half to three hours of babysitting a day. The advantage to this arrangement is that parents aren't always watching the clock, and sitters are assured a regular wage they can count on, even when there are fewer hours of work.

LIVE-IN VS. LIVE-OUT

We're thinking of hiring a woman who worked as a live-in for friends of ours. We want her to live-out, which I've heard is more a expensive proposition. Do we have to top her old salary?

Conventionally, live-ins get less cash because room and board is provided; live-outs receive about five to ten percent more because they must maintain a separate residence, though many live-ins have homes and families they return to on the weekends. The loophole lies in the length of the day. If, in her live-in job, the nanny got up with the kids at seven and put them to sleep at eight, you're talking a thirteen-hour day—unlikely you'd be asking a live-out for the same thing. If you do require the same long hours, then there's no reasonable way out of topping her former salary. Except to say you simply can't—then the ball is in her court.

OVERTIME AND OVERNIGHTS

When my wife and I go out at night, we prefer to ask our regular nanny to stay late than to scramble around for a different evening sitter. The problem is price: She wants fourteen dollars an hour instead of her usual eight. Suddenly, a simple evening out becomes an expensive proposition.

Nearly double may sound like a lot—and it is—but it really depends on each individual's situation. For the nanny who's already worked a long day, and is anxious to get home to see her kids or meet up with friends, another two or three hours at her regular (or close to it) rate is probably not temptation enough to stay at work. And if you're asking her to sit on a weekend night, and she lives at some distance, making the effort to come in to work for a few hours in the evening may also call for more enticement. (It's de rigueur to pay for transportation home at night). Of course, even if you think her fee is justified it may still be too much dough to cough up just to see a movie. In that case, you can propose you split the difference—say, eleven dollars an hour. It may well be worth it for you to pay extra for the ease and convenience of a known entity (no going through the where-everything-is routine, no listening to your kids throw screaming tantrums with a stranger). If she won't budge, time to increase your pool of evening sitters.

I need to take an out-of-town business trip during the week and want our sitter to stay overnight. It seems excessive to pay her normal rate for the entire time she's sleeping, but I want to make staying over worth her while.

While the range is wide, the majority of parents pay between fifty to seventy dollars extra for the night. However, if you're talking about newborns or infants who still aren't sleeping through the night—or if you have three or more kids—then seventy-five to a hundred is more the norm. There's also the issue of when the overnight ends and the next day's work begins. Some parents calculate it this way: They pay the nanny's usual hourly wage up until midnight and resume it again at six in the morning, or whenever the kids are likely to get up.

ACCOUNTING FOR EXTRAS

Our nanny just started with us, and at the end of the month, she handed over an itemized bill totaling one hundred and sixty dollars for her commuting costs—train fare, and cabs to and

from the station. She says her previous employers have always covered transportation—but we never talked about it.

There's an even split among parents here: Half are happy to pay commuting costs, half see it as the nanny's responsibility (on the theory that their own employers don't reimburse *them* for getting to and from work). If the sitter's commute is particularly long and complicated, consider the fact that she has to start her day that much earlier to get to you on time—and help her defray the cost, if only by fifty percent. But whatever arrangement you make, be sure it's clear—this is one of those murky money areas that left unresolved can derail a relationship.

I found out recently that my sitter hangs out with a "rich nanny" clique—they take the kids out to eat all the time, and not to inexpensive places. My nanny's been asking for more petty cash. I don't want to exclude her or my kids from the group, but it's getting out of hand.

Petty cash is typically a small amount of money stashed in an envelope to cover incidentals like taxis, milk, or tickets to a movie. But as in every walk of life, there are high spenders and tight wads. Just set your limits. Tell the nanny how much you're comfortable giving her for the week, and tell her to use it wisely. If she wants to save up for the rich-nanny lunch once or twice a week, fine—they'll have to eat peanut butter sandwiches the other days. If you want to police the types of places they're going, that's a whole other agenda, and calls for a conversation not about how they're spending their money, but about how they're spending their time.

DOCKING PAY AND SWAPPING HOURS

For the last two weeks, the babysitter has been an hour late— she's caught up in red tape trying to transfer her daughter to a different school. The first week I was understanding and let it go. Now I feel I should start deducting the hours from her weekly pay.

Lots of parents find themselves in a quandary over what to do when missed hours here and there start adding up. Rather than lopping hours off her pay, which may lead to hardship for her and make a bad situation worse, try to take the long view. If the relationship between you is good, you trust her motivations are sincere, and she assures you that the situation is short-term, then it's a good policy to pay in full—up to a point: After a week, there's nothing wrong with asking her to make up some of the missed hours. The rule of thumb about bargaining: Divide by two. Ask for half of the missed hours to be "paid back" in the form of a late night or a weekend afternoon.

When my grandfather died recently, I told the nanny I'd be taking the kids to the funeral for the day. I added, casually, that she could make up the time by babysitting one night the following week. She looked down and said, tight-lipped, that it wasn't fair. I was surprised, because my request seemed more than fair—an extra two or three hours in exchange for a day off.

Easy for the novice parent to misunderstand and easy for the nanny to get her feathers ruffled up over. The guiding principle: If you make a change in the schedule, you still pay—*she* didn't ask not to work. And this rule applies across the board, whether you're talking about an afternoon off to take the kids to the museum, or a spontaneous two-day family trip. The exception is if you give the caregiver at least a week's notice, and you both agree that she'll use that time off as one of her vacation days. Of course if she'd rather save her vacation days to use in one lump, then you should just pay up.

Our nanny needs to fly home to Barbados—a hurricane has blown the roof off her mother's house—and will be gone a week. Whose pocket does this come out of?

Strictly speaking, hers. Time off for family emergencies—anything from caring for a sick child to nursing an elderly parent to getting through a divorce—should be taken as sick days or vacation days. If she's used those days up, advance her some from next year. You could also treat the time as an unpaid leave—not a bad strategy if you have any reason to believe that once she leaves, she won't come back. Still, a lot of employers cover anywhere from half to all of the salary of a temporarily indisposed nanny, depending on how close (and how flush) they feel.

Overheard: The Nanny Who Wouldn't Go Home

I should have been happy about this, but it irked me: Our sitter was paid to stay until six o'clock, but four out of five days she'd hang around an extra hour, doing dishes, folding laundry, and chatting with the kids. She never asked for more money, but I felt guilty and would often throw in an extra twenty or thirty dollars at the end of the week. Her salary was creeping up without us having discussed it. I couldn't take the ambiguity anymore. Finally, I asked her if she wanted to officially work until 7:00. I figured if she said no, she'd get the message and leave closer to six o'clock, and I would certainly be absolved of paying her.

If she said yes, I was willing to add the hour. As it turned out, she wanted to stay, and used that hour to start the family dinner, which took an enormous load off my shoulders. Before this, it hadn't occurred to me what that extra hour of help at that time of evening could mean. The new deal was good for everyone.

A Quick Study: On or Off the Books

Why is it that so many otherwise intelligent, law-abiding citizens choose to skirt the nanny tax (about 75 percent, say accountants)? There are a few compelling reasons: Paying on the books costs you more as the employer because you have to pay Social Security and unemployment taxes; filing the paperwork four times a year can be a hassle; and many nannies insist on all cash to avoid paying taxes themselves. In fact, paying on the books has gotten a bad rap, but it's not *that* complicated. And for the nanny there are actually some advantages long term. She stands to gain security—she's eligible for unemployment, Social Security benefits, and disability. Plus, she may one day need those returns to establish credit or substantiate income for major purchases or loans.

Here's the deal, in the simplest possible terms. Both you and the sitter are responsible for taxes: You, as the employer, pay about 10 or 11 percent of your nanny's annual salary (depending on your state)—this number covers unemployment insurance, plus half of her Social Security and Medicare payments (she pays the other half), and any miscellaneous state taxes. And your nanny, as the employee, pays annual taxes ranging from 15 to 20 percent of her salary—this covers her portion of Social Security and Medicare; her federal and state taxes, plus any miscellaneous taxes, such as disability. Employers are required to withhold the nanny's share of Social Security and Medicare from her paycheck, and remit the money to the government on her behalf at tax time. Typically, employers offer to withhold the sitter's federal and state taxes as well, so she doesn't have to worry about saving for the tax bill.

A sample scenario plays out like this: Say your nanny makes $350 a week; that's a gross annual salary of $18,200. You, the employer, will have to pay, on average, an annual 10 percent in taxes, or $1,820, which essentially means that your childcare costs jump from $350 to $385 a week. Your nanny's annual taxes and Social Security payments will come out to about $2,730, depending on the state in which she lives and how many exemptions she claims on her W-4 form. That amount of money withheld weekly results in a paycheck of $297.50 (if you withhold only the Social Security and Medicare, the check would be $323.23). Because in either scenario the paycheck comes to less than an all-cash deal, some parents will tack on a little more money in cash to compensate. You do get a little bit of a break— two federal tax breaks, that is. The first is a childcare credit you can claim on your 1040 that allows you to deduct up to fourteen hundred dollars from your total income. The second is a benefit offered by many company plans that allows you to set aside up to five thousand in pre-tax dollars for childcare, which reduces your year-end income for tax purposes.

As far as paperwork goes, you—or your accountant—must file federal and state taxes quarterly. You must also request tax ID numbers from the state and IRS—call your regional offices for the application. The IRS estimates that it takes forty hours to fill out the forms, which is why the majority of people ask for help. You can pay an accountant to do it for you (the average fee is six hundred dollars a year; less if you go to an agency that specializes in this field) or you can invest in software for about a hundred and fifty dollars that makes do-it-yourself a little more doable.

Chapter 5

Raising the Stakes

The raise is an unspoken part of the package, implicit in the deal. It's expected, but the when, why, and how much is not always self-evident. Although as employers we give a lot of thought to a caregiver's starting salary and put the number right out there on the table, we often don't think through (much less talk about) the issue of the raise. One reason may be that parents don't want to feel obligated to dole out a raise if things go south with a given sitter. Many find it easier simply to present the salary increase as a fait accompli without having let any expectations build up. But there's a persuasive argument for an early, spoken promise of a specific pay hike, to be given after a certain period of employment: There's no chance of disappointment or hemming and hawing. The nanny won't be hoping for more, and you won't be conflicted about how much to give. And if the nanny outdoes herself, you can always bump up the raise—a nice surprise.

As for what's standard and respectable, annual raises range from 5 to 10 percent of the weekly salary (at the very least a raise should cover the increase in cost of living). Most people use the percentage as a gauge, then round up—say, by twenty-five or thirty dollars a week. But before you're knee-jerk generous, think ahead. Let's say you decide to give a sitter a fifty dollars per week raise every year: After three years, you'd be committed to a $150 jump in salary ($7,800 more annually). It's smarter to promise raises in smaller increments than to have to reduce the raises, or stop them altogether.

Another unwritten, unnegotiated benefit is the holiday bonus—on average, a week's salary (two, for longterm employees), given near the end of the year. It's a quirk of the nanny field that, unlike the traditional company bonus, this monetary perk is not normally tied to job performance but rather is given as a matter of course. (Certainly, like businesses that are having a good year, parents who are feeling flush—and happy with the sitter—may choose to share the "profits"). While the majority of employers simply give their nannies money, there are those who are put off by the idea of handing out cold hard cash, seeing it in the same category as an end-of-year payoff to the doorman or garbage man. Rather, these families prefer to give a tangible gift. But in order for a present to be "meaningful"—and replace a bonus—it should be substantial, worth something in the region of a week's salary. In some instances, a gift ends up being even more valuable, as in a roundtrip plane ticket home to visit family over the holidays— generous in deed and spirit.

While money is almost always complicated, emotionally and practically, loans are a particularly tricky matter. When a sitter comes to you with a specific need (to get a kid medical treatment or bail a relative out of jail), it's natural to want to help out. But nannies and loans, just like families and loans, tend not to mix too well. What happens when payments are late, checks bounce, and you find yourself wondering why she isn't paying you back yet seems to have a lot of new clothes? And there's always the possibility, however remote, of the cut-and-run, never-to-be-heard-of again scenario. If you decide, however, that you're going to give (or give in), the best strategy is to be crystal clear about the terms. Otherwise, you'll find yourself letting her off the hook financially, even if you never forget or forgive.

THE SALARY BUMP

My friend just raised her nanny's salary—after only six months. I was planning on giving an increase after a year. What's the protocol?

There are two schools of thought about raises. The most common is to bump a salary annually, starting roughly a year after the nanny was hired. The second approach is to raise early and often, doing, say, the first review at three months, another at six months, a third after a year, and annually thereafter. The benefit of this technique is that it gives you built-in, multiple review times, during which you can discuss small course corrections without having to wrap up the whole year in one Big Talk. You'll be out a bit more money sooner, of course, but you'll end up in the same place, raising your sitter an average of five to ten percent annually.

It's been almost a year since we hired our nanny and I'm sure she expects a raise. I'm loath to give it, though, because in fact I'm not thrilled with her habit of being late and calling in sick. Is a raise mandatory?

Withholding a raise sends a strong message. If you don't give even a token increase, you're inviting her either to start looking for another job or to start resenting you (which, in turn, could backlash on the kids). You could always defer the expected full raise— give her a warning period of, say, three months—and then revisit the issue. But unless your nanny is unusually self-possessed, and able to put aside indignation, you're probably in for three tense, testy months. If you want her to stay, in the hope that she'll become more dependable, think about a small raise, say, ten dollars a week—with the promise of a further increase when she gets her act together.

Our sitter came to me the other day and asked me for a raise, although it's not time for her yearly bump. She said she can't make it on the salary we're giving her, and that she needs fifty dollars more a week or she'll have to move on. I feel a little backed into a corner.

If she comes asking, she probably really needs it and will have to look for another job—though nannies, like employees in any industry, have been known to bluff, whether it's by claiming a better (and phantom) offer from another family, or the need for money for a so-called emergency surgery that never seems to be performed. Assuming she's telling the truth, however, applaud her chutzpah. As for the raise, you have to make a decision about how valuable she is to you. If you can afford the increase, let her know that the new yearly raise cycle begins from this point forward.

Nanny Point of View: The Low-Ball Raise

"It's amazing to me that parents will spend extravagantly on toys and clothes for the kids, on interior designers and architects, on horseback-riding lessons, and they'll snap their wallets shut when it comes to giving nannies a raise. It's hard not to expect more than a token raise when we see so much money being thrown around. If caregivers are so important, why don't employers make us feel like we are?"

THE INVISIBLE INCREASE

On our nanny's one-year anniversary with us, we plan to give her a raise, which will come to $25 more a week. The hitch is that we've also just decided to put her on the books as a household employee, which means that by the time we withhold taxes, her take-home pay will actually go down and the raise will be lost.

This is a bind that parents who belatedly decide to "go legal" often face. From where the nanny sits, the new plan is probably not looking so good: She took the job at a certain income with the understanding that an annual raise would bump it up, not down; to change the plan, at your discretion, seems unfair. But to you, the employer, who will suddenly be paying her taxes, your taxes, and perhaps accountant's fees, the raise is plenty fair. If twenty-five dollars more is your limit, you have to stick with it, and explain where the raise is going—for starters, into her own Social Security fund. If you feel compelled to adjust her take-home pay to equal the amount she would have made in an all-cash arrangement, you'll have to nearly double your intended raise—to fifty dollars. Whatever the decision, make it clear this is a one-time-only adjustment. Next year, it's business as usual.

HITTING THE SALARY CEILING

We've been lucky enough to have a superb nanny for five years—and have given her a 10-percent raise each spring. That means her salary has increased by 50 percent since she started. Where do we stop?

It's perfectly reasonable to put a cap on a salary. In fact, at a point where you feel you're paying substantially more than the market, it's only logical. After all, unlike in other industries where salaries are commensurate with increases in job responsibilities, in this business the job remains pretty much constant (unless you have more children, dramatically change the hours, or add other household tasks—in which case you would adjust the wage). What you can do is slow down to a very small raise or a raise every other year, and reward her in other ways—with more vacation time or days off. In any case, take comfort in the fact that after five years with you, your sitter is making a far higher wage than she would be if she started over with a new family.

Bonus Points

I handed our nanny a fat envelope with her weekly salary plus an extra week's salary as a bonus. It's been several days and she hasn't said a thing. I wonder if she's disappointed.

Although a bonus is routine, it can carry a lot of emotional weight. Parents see the money as a gift, and feel they're being generous, so they expect some show of thanks in return. Nannies sometimes seem underwhelmed, giving the impression (perhaps false) that they were expecting more. Sometimes they are, but just as often they got what they expected, and feel no more need to show appreciation than they do for their weekly salary. There's the possibility, too, that the nanny is simply shy about expressing gratitude, or uncomfortable talking money in any guise. If the sitter is truly disappointed by her bonus, you'll probably be able to detect a sour note in her behavior, which can open the door for a what-were-you-hoping-for discussion. But if she keeps coming in smiling, assume all is well.

I know it's de rigeur to give a yearly bonus, but we pay top-dollar in salary, and since we travel frequently, our nanny gets four or five weeks of paid vacation at the very least. It seems excessive to add to the benefits.

True, in the nanny profession a lump-sum cash bonus has come to be expected. But that doesn't mean a bonus is by any means required. It's just one part of the pay package, and if the other parts—vacation, salary, holidays—are more than generous, there's no reason to feel bad about stinting on or skipping the perk. In fact, some employers use the bonus as a way of assuaging their guilt over not paying a higher salary—it's a once-a-year splurge that they feel (and hope) compensates for middle-of-the-road pay. If a week's salary is simply too extravagant, a gift can at least show appreciation—and make a nanny feel valued.

We're feeling pinched and can't really afford to pay a bonus this year. But the last thing we need to do is to offend—or lose—our caregiver.

If your nanny is happy, chances are slim you're going to lose her over a week's salary. But to offset the chance that she might misinterpret your action as disappointment in her performance, be up front about your reasons. Don't assume she can surmise that just because you're working two jobs and have pulled your kids out of private school, it means there's less money all around for everyone. Anytime families expect nannies to read between the lines—"can't she see we're strapped?"—there's room for misunderstanding. And no matter how cash-crunched you are, make some gesture—whether it's a few extra days off around the holidays or a modest present—so that your actions match your words.

Nanny Point of View: A Birthday Sentiment

"I always remember the birthdays of the children I'm taking care of, and when my employer remembers my birthday, it makes me feel flattered and appreciated. More than the money spent, I want to think they put thought into the gift. I once got a pair of tickets to a professional basketball game, which I loved. But the best present I ever got was a home-baked cake from the children and the entire day off."

THE LOAN QUANDARY

Our nanny seemed on the verge of tears all day, and when I finally asked if everything was all right, she blurted out that her house would be foreclosed unless she came up with $5,000 by the day after tomorrow. Then she dropped the other shoe: Could we loan her the money?

Even if you can come up with money on such short notice, a loan can bring an emotional price. The nanny may feel beholden and you may feel burdened. On the other hand, by not loaning her the money, you may be putting her in a perilous spot, one in which her own financial woes and entanglements overtake her ability to work for you. If you do decide to play banker, however, you're in a position to garner a portion of her salary—a given amount every month—which may well make sense with this much money at stake. But if any part of you doubts she'll stick around to pay you back, bow out and accept the potential consequences.

Nanny Point of View: The Favor that Wasn't

"My boss always told me I could come to him if I needed anything. Anything at all, he said. Well, the one time I did really did need his help—I asked to borrow money to get my kids new winter coats—he showed his true colors. All he was concerned about was asking me all sorts of questions that made me feel like I was under an inquisition, like how much was my rent and how many credit cards did I carry. After he grilled me for a while, he finally said okay, he'd loan me the money. But by then, I decided I would do anything rather than accept money from him. I thought he was two-faced."

It's definitely in our interest for our nanny to get a car—we've been picking her up and dropping her off at the train station each day, a true inconvenience. But since she doesn't have much credit of her own, she's asked us to co-sign her loan. We're mixed . . .

This is that rare situation in which a loan pays off for you, too. If you're inclined to help, you may be better off arranging a private (i.e., no banks involved) transaction yourself; otherwise, if she's late with any of her payments, then your name—and credit—is smeared and you'll need to jump through hoops to get it corrected. If you've got the means, loan her a portion of what she needs—say, five hundred or a thousand dollars—so she can borrow less from a bank, and do it on the basis of her own credit. That way you can completely extricate yourself from her financial future.

Overheard: A Taxing Situation

When it came time for our sitter to pay her taxes, she was way short on cash and approached us for help. It turns out she'd never been paid on the books before, and although we thought we'd made it clear that she'd be responsible for her share of Social Security and federal taxes, she didn't really understand what that meant in dollars and cents. So she asked us if we could lend her $1,200. I told her I'd think about it, but my instinct was no—she'd been warned and if she couldn't figure out how to save the money herself, it wasn't our problem. But then, as my husband and I talked about it, we thought about how easy it is to come up short at tax time, especially since this was all new to her. We remembered how, even when we knew we needed to save money for something, our habits didn't always follow our good intentions. We decided to cut her some slack. The next day, the three of us sat down and talked about the best way for her to pay us back. She proposed we deduct $100 from her pay every other week—and in six months, we'd have our money back. She offered to add interest, but we thought that was unnecessary. After all, it was due to our insistence on going legal that her financial picture became so complicated. In fact, as we talked further, we decided we'd pay for her visits to her accountant, too—just for this year.

Chapter 6

Days Off—Official and Otherwise

A vacation isn't an arbitrary notion. It probably shouldn't even be considered a perk—everyone knows that a little R&R is good for one's soul and one's job performance. And in the caregiver's line of work, paid vacation time is expected; it's right there, in the unwritten book of rules: A full-time sitter (one who works twenty-five hours or more a week) is entitled to at least five days a year. Most employers give two weeks right off the bat, and they go up to three after five years. But "typical" has wide margins, depending on individual schedules. Families who take lengthy summer or holiday vacations—for two, three, four weeks at a stretch—often pay their nannies for that time too, making her total vacation package more like five or six weeks a year. In those cases, an arrangement is sometimes made for the sitter to "house-watch" or do light cleaning in the employers' absence.

Regardless, the vacation policy should be worked out up front, during the negotiation-hiring stage, with a clear understanding about who decides when the sitter is to take her vacation—an often divisive issue between nannies and employers. A sitter, like most employees, should be allowed to schedule her own days off, with enough advance warning to the boss. But for obvious reasons, most employers prefer to have the nanny plan her vacation around theirs: They don't have to pay her while she's gone another one or two weeks, and there's no need to get back-up help or miss work. Some parents make it very clear from the start, as part of the offer, that the nanny *must* take her vacation when the family does, and that in addition, she can have up to two weeks off as unpaid leave whenever she wishes. What usually satisfies everyone, however, is a half-and-half arrangement: The nanny chooses half her days; the parents the other.

Time off also comes wrapped up as holidays, which seem to pop up every month or so, affording parents more opportunities to fret over schedules and their own sense of generosity. To give or not to give—that is the question that most of us grapple with. All the major holidays go without saying: Christmas, New Year's Day, Thanksgiving, and Fourth of July. Thanksgiving and Christmas often come with extra days, gratis, particularly if the parents are taking those days off from work or going away for the holidays. Memorial Day and Labor Day are considered second-tier and are typically given off as well, and unless you stipulate otherwise, nannies usually expect them. Where things get murky is with the third-tier holidays, or "optionals": Columbus Day, Veterans Day, Presidents' Day, Martin Luther King Day, and Good Friday. Working parents who don't get these days off themselves often don't give them in turn. A good strategy is to allow a choice of one or two (or more) of the minor holidays a year.

When it comes to sick days, most employers adopt the we'll-cross-that-bridge-when-we-come-to-it attitude. This nonstrategy usually works out fine, but it's not a bad idea to agree on a set number for the year—you'll avoid potentially uncomfortable decisions about whether or not to pay each time the sitter misses work. A good gauge is one day for each day of the week she works (five days a year for a five-day week; three for three, etc). True, a sitter who knows she's allotted a specific number of days may be tempted to take the time even when she's not really sick, though one could also argue that a mental health day now and then might in fact be legitimate. It's also smart to discuss what you and the sitter can work out if she happens to get sick for more than a few days in a row. First, in terms of backup: Does she have a sister? friends who could cover? And then in terms of salary: It's more than fair to pay a sick caregiver for a week after her sick days are used; beyond that, however, it's perfectly reasonable to stop paying, or to pay and ask her to make up the hours when she's well.

One of the foggiest areas has to do with personal time off. A day to go to a funeral or deal with a household emergency (the bathroom ceiling's caved in) is not usually docked, but should the nanny have to leave the country for a period, or take a leave of absence to care for an ill relative, the one-week rule still holds. (Parents who are devoted to their sitters may keep up the salary, in the belief that it all works out on balance—they have a vested interest in the sitter and are convinced she's coming back.) But let's say the tables are turned and it's you who changes the routine—you decide one morning to take the kids to the circus for the day, or you go off to a family wedding. In those cases, she shouldn't have to make up the hours. It's not that she's taking the time off—you're giving it.

VACATION TIME AND TIMING

We started our sitter off with two weeks of vacation, then added another week after she'd been with us three years. We can't keep racking up the weeks or we'll have no childcare.

Vacations, like raises, are often capped—a nanny who has been with you five years should not be expecting five weeks off. If you feel it doesn't work for your family to give more than two or three weeks of vacation (and for many working families, it simply doesn't), a perfectly reasonable alternative is to bump the yearly raise a little more instead—in lieu of vacation, you may offer her an extra ten dollars per week. That's worth $520 per year, probably more than her one week's paid vacation would amount to anyway.

When we hired our nanny, we mentioned that our family always took off the last two weeks of August. I thought she understood—and agreed—but now it turns out she wants to take her two weeks this spring.

The question of who calls the vacation shots can cause a lot of friction. You declared your intention, but she may have assumed that she was still free to take her two weeks whenever. Insisting that a caregiver twist her life to fit yours doesn't always work. Some nannies have a lot of flexibility and are happy to accommodate their employers, others *have* to plan family vacations around their kids' school breaks. A typical compromise is to ask her to take one of her two weeks while you're away. Without some give and take, one side has to give in completely, which leaves the other party feeling stranded.

Our sitter only works three days a week. Are we still expected to give vacation days?

There's a fine line with part-timers and it's drawn at the three-day-a-week mark. At that level or more, the same vacation logic applies; as with full-timers one or two weeks the first year, and so on. For sitters who work only one or two days a week, paid vacation is rare. Ditto for paid holidays—if one falls on a sitter's workday, it makes sense to simply switch the day for another that week. The conventional rules don't always apply, however, in the case of a close relationship with a long-term part-timer; an employer may feel, for instance, like saying, "skip this holiday week and enjoy yourself."

TRICKY TRADES

We'll be gone for two weeks at Christmas and the nanny has already used up her vacation time. We've agreed to pay her in full for the weeks we're gone but have asked her to come in a few hours a day to clean out the kitchen cabinets and to reorganize the playroom. She clearly isn't thrilled—but we feel it's more than fair.

This is one of those issues that can be argued from either side. A lot of nannies feel that their only job is to take care of the children—and if those kids are away, they're not needed. Why, they legitimately wonder, should they suddenly be switched to a housekeeper role? (Babysitters who already have housecleaning in their job description are usually not as prickly, as long as they're being paid in full.) From the parents' point of view, the light-workload arrangement is a pretty good deal for the sitter: two weeks of pay for a couple of hours of work a day. If you're not sure if she'll balk or not, bring the matter up for discussion. And if she seems amenable to a "Do you mind doing a few projects around the house . . ." request, then ask her for suggestions—she's less likely to be grumpy about the whole deal.

Nanny Point of View: The Reluctant Housesitter

"I expect my regular salary when my employers are away. It's their choice not to use my services at that time. If I was asked to do chores or show up to house-sit while they were away, it would bother me because that is not part of my job. I'm certain if the roles were reversed, and they were given time off from their employment, that they wouldn't have to go in and clean their office or do busy work just because they were still getting a paycheck."

Our longtime sitter has three weeks of vacation time, which she usually takes to fly home to Costa Rica. This year she asked if she could have the cash—about a thousand dollars—rather than the time off. I feel mixed about it.

A vacation really benefits everyone: The sitter gets a break, comes back refreshed, staves off burnout—all of which trickles down to kids and parents. If you think about it, a whole year without a stretch of time off can be exhausting. On the other hand, almost everyone has years like this, and survives. And life throws people loops—she may have no choice but to ask for the cash. In terms of money, you're not paying any more if you were planning to hire a replacement anyway. If not, and you were planning to fill in yourself, then it comes down to a financial decision which you may have to negotiate—including the proviso that this is a one-time-only deal.

Our family plans to spend July at the beach and the sitter has to stay behind in the city with her young children. Rather than have her miss out on four weeks of salary, I found her a month's employment with a friend in town. I thought she'd be happy, but she seems miffed.

She's probably miffed at being handed off. Even though you think you're doing her a favor by finding her work, it may be presumptuous to assume she hasn't made alternate plans and would even want to work for your friend. And just because you've lined up a potential gig for her in your absence doesn't in any way let you off the hook in terms of paying her salary. She's entitled to a full 52 weeks of pay, whether you're there or not. The best you can do is ask her to use some portion of her vacation time, whether it's one, two, or three weeks, during your month off.

HOLIDAYS, MAJOR AND MINOR

I never know what to do when it comes to bank holidays—I don't get them off from my job, so practically speaking, I can't really afford to give them to my sitter. But since her kids are usually home from school those days, I'm putting her out.

If you were to give each and every quasi-holiday with pay, you'd find your sitter would be taking a paid holiday once a month. A common solution is to come up with a set number—say two or three—optional holidays (in the category that includes Presidents' Day, Memorial Day, etc.) that the nanny can take in addition to The Big Four (Thanksgiving, Christmas, New Year's Day, and The Fourth of July). This way, each time a questionable holiday comes up you eliminate those uncomfortable conversations in which you feel like a miser for asking her to work, and she feels rooked for not getting the day off. As for the school dilemma, if she doesn't have convenient or easy backup, one solution is have her bring her own kid(s) to work with her on these few-and-far-between days.

My nanny told me that in the past, she was given off the entire week between Christmas and New Year. I'd like to be so generous, but I really need help during that time.

Not every family can afford to give the nanny time off that week unless they themselves are heading out of town. Assuming that's not the case, it's perfectly legit to ask her to come in. Just be clear. Ambiguity—as in, "We'll see how the week goes"—is tough to live with and plan around. And if you present your limitations up front—as in, "I'd love to give you more time, but I work that week," or "I have to recover from the onslaught of my in-laws"—then she's not apt to view any stinginess as singular or personal. If you can, try to throw in an extra few hours off in the spirit of the season: a half day for holiday shopping or the afternoon of New Year's Eve; such a seemingly small gesture conveys your good intentions.

We're having a huge family gathering for Thanksgiving, and although I would normally give our sitter the day off, I really need her to watch the kids while I prepare the meal. If she agrees, how do I handle pay?

Since it's a holiday, and presumably she'll be sacrificing her own family time, you have to make it worth her while. General rule of thumb: Double her hourly rate. And for the sake of your future relationship, ask her in such a way that she doesn't feel obliged— "only if you want to" or "let me know once you've thought about it." A lot of employees feel they have to say yes to stay in your good graces. But the last thing you want is to make her feel forced into working—which would be no holiday for anyone.

Martin Luther King Day is coming up, and when my nanny reminded me she wouldn't be coming in that day, I was taken aback. Apparently I gave her the day off last year, but I'd forgotten—and this year I'm in the middle of a deadline and I'm not prepared to stay home.

It's tricky to have to renegotiate what's paid from year to year, especially if each of you remembers it a little differently. Ideally, this is the kind of stuff you'd have worked out at the hiring stage. If not, do it now. Spell out on paper how many of the minor holidays you're willing to give off, with input from her about which ones she'd like. Switching the days around—trading Veterans Day for Columbus Day—is no big deal as long as she gives you ample notice, and as long as the overall number of days remains steady. And you can always offer to pay her more if you're stuck and need her to work on what you'd agreed would be a paid holiday. For time-and-a-half, she may be more than willing.

SNOW DAYS AND SICK DAYS

We live in a place where it snows. A lot. Our sitter, who is from the South, freaks out at the first flake, and several times she's called to say she's afraid to drive in snowy weather. I've still got to make it to my office, so I feel that if she can't make it here, we shouldn't pay.

You should probably still pay her (unless her combined snow-and-sick days tops five) but you've definitely got an issue to work out if you feel that her reticence is psychological. When you find yourself wondering why the rest of the world can brave the weather, it's only natural to question why she can't get from there to here. You don't want to suddenly become her shrink, so if you sense her fear of driving is truly phobic, you may have to think about practical alternative measures. You could offer to have her stay over with you (room permitting) when bad weather is predicted, or arrange for a car service to take her back and forth (you can split the cost). Those winters when nature goes really wild, and everyone is plowed under for days at a time, its only fair to increase the allotted snow days.

Our sitter tends to get ill for weeks at a time during flu season. Even if she comes to work, she's not all there. It's not that I mind paying her for sick days (although she always exceeds them); I just want her to be able to function.

Some employers, particularly those who are very committed to their nannies, solve this problem out of pocket by covering some or all of the cost of preventative care, including yearly physicals, mammograms, pap smears, and flu shots for both the nanny and

her children. A few families go so far as to subsidize health insurance for their employees or add them to their own plans, since
many nannies have inadequate coverage (au pairs, by the way,
are typically covered by their sponsoring agencies). These parents
justify the cost, rightly so, by saying the nanny's health is critical
to the well-being of the entire family.

**Before we had a live-in, a sick day was a sick day. Now it's
harder to draw the line. Our nanny hasn't taken an official day
off, but she's had a whole slew of "sick afternoons."**

It's hard to know whether you come out ahead or behind with a
live-in—the balance can tip either way, depending on her temperament. With a sitter who takes to bed, or takes to complaining, at the least sniffle or stomach cramp, you may have to set
clear rules about when she's on or off duty, since your home is
also her infirmary. A conscientious type, on the other hand, will
work through a minor illness—and at eighty percent; while she
may not be up to roughhousing, she's perfectly capable of picking
up the kids at school. Unfortunately, the do-gooder nanny may
push herself until she's quite ill, simply because she *is* there, de-
nying herself the needed rest. Make it clear she's entitled to a few
bona fide sick days—and that she doesn't have to grab get-well
hours on the fly. Give her license occasionally to "call in" sick,
and assure her that one of you (or whomever) will cover for her
and let her off the hook for the entire day.

**I fear we have a hypochondriac on our hands. In the last six
weeks, our nanny has missed work for a sprained ankle, migraine headaches, and various gastric ailments. Should I start
docking her?**

Only if she exceeds a reasonable number of sick days. If you
don't set a limit, then each illness or injury becomes a separate

negotiation. Should you pay for strep throat? Or the migraine? Once she's hit her quota, five days or so, you can simply tell her you can't pay for any more missed work. Something else to think about: Perhaps her complaints are less about illness and more about the work itself. Could it be she's looking for a way out? Another job? Maybe this is the only way she knows how to gripe.

Overheard: Calling in Sick—on Day One

We'd decided to hire a new sitter right before Christmas and she graciously offered to start the next day, which happened to be the day I was throwing a big holiday party. At 7:30 the next morning, however, the phone rang. The sitter was calling in sick. Even though it's not very nice, my first thought was, There go the day's plans right out the window. My husband heard me take the call. I could see him rolling his eyes, as if to say, Oh great. But I liked the way she handled the situation. She said, "I have a dilemma. I started throwing up in the middle of the night. I haven't been sick again since 4 A.M. and I don't want to let you down, but I'm tired and I don't want to risk infecting your kids, especially right before Christmas. What would you like me to do?" In a way, it was a rhetorical question—of course she should stay home. But by even bothering to ask for my opinion, she gave me a good feeling about the way she approaches a predicament. Our nine-year-old daughter, a true cynic, was convinced that the sitter was bluffing and just wanted to hang with her boyfriend, who she'd mentioned was visiting from out of town. And when the sitter finally did start, the following week, it was our daughter who kept pressing her for the details, trying to find holes in her story. Not me—she'd already won me over.

A QUICK STUDY: WORKERS' COMP (OR HOW NOT TO GET SUED)

What would happen if your nanny were to slip down the stairs on the way to the laundry room or put her back out while giving the kids a horsey ride? Who pays her salary while she's out of commission? Who covers what could be substantial medical costs? Simple questions with tricky answers. About half of all the states require employers to purchase workers' compensation for domestic employees. Namely: California, Colorado, Connecticut, Delaware, Hawaii, Illinois, Iowa, Kansas, Kentucky, Maryland, Massachusetts, Michigan, Minnesota, New Hampshire, New York, Ohio, Oklahoma, South Carolina, South Dakota, Utah, and Washington, as well as the District of Columbia. In some states, workers' comp is required for nannies working a minimum of sixteen hours per week; others stipulate forty hours and up per week. Check with your state's Department of Labor or your insurance agent to find out where your state stands. Workers' comp covers a nanny's medical bills and physical rehab, and replaces her lost wages (usually at two-thirds the rate)—and it does so regardless (and this is key) of who's at fault. That means, for example, if you neglected to tack down the carpeting that she later tripped over, you're not responsible.

You buy workers' comp through your regular insurance agent, who arranges for a rider on your homeowner's/renter's policy at an added cost of anywhere from one to three hundred dollars a year. But what if your state doesn't require you to carry workers' comp—what then? Most parents, truth be told, don't bother to add any extra insurance at all, assuming that their general household policy will be coverage enough—and usually it is. It probably makes sense to buy the rider if you suspect you have a litigious sitter and if you have a fair amount of wealth or property you want to protect. Then, if the nanny sues over that loose carpeting, you've got yourself, and your assets, covered.

Part III

Division of Labor

Chapter 7

Sorting out the Laundry and Other Household Chores

It's a given that a sitter is going to take care of the children. But many of us hire a nanny with the hope that she's going to take care of the house—and us, too. Parents who tend to wax most ecstatic about their babysitters report that they feel nurtured or pampered in some way: They come home to a clean house, the children fed and bathed, the laundry folded, the beds made, dinner cooking on the stove. Granted that's the ideal, but any version or part of that scenario is worth a lot to most parents, especially harried ones. And a little household help is not an unreasonable wish. Most nannies are more than willing to take on a few chores when the kids are asleep or out of the house (or even underfoot). But since many of these tasks fall into the category of "above-and-beyond"—particularly if you haven't spelled them out as part of the job description—you ought to be diplomatic in the asking and show gratitude in the receiving.

The childrens' laundry, everyone seems to agree, does come with the territory. And if the nanny has the time—more than an hour or two free a day—it's perfectly kosher to ask her to throw in the family's wash as well. In many households, everyone's laundry is comingled anyway; if so, the nanny simply gets done what she can get done, even if that's only a dent in the pile. No nanny should be expected to be a full-time laundress. If you have major wash—you like the sheets changed twice a week and the table linens ironed—then you should probably think about hiring another hand.

When it comes to shopping and stocking the refrigerator, the nanny is typically responsible for the essentials, like milk, bread, baby food, diapers. Even if she can't get out to replace them, she should let you know when you're running low. As for the general family shopping, if both parents work late and can't make it to the store and home by the sitter's leaving time, then it's in everyone's interest to have her do the daily or weekly food runs; and along the way, she can pick up what she likes to eat and drink, too.

As for cooking, a nanny should be able to at least get a kid's meals on the table, even if that means frozen pizza. If she happens to be an accomplished cook (purees vegetables for the baby, bakes oatmeal cookies with the older kids, and prepares homemade stews for the family), that's gravy. Of course, the nanny who spends *too* much time in the kitchen may be leaving other chores undone—such as the kids' laundry, lying crumpled in the basket. If you care, you need to work out a better balance with her.

Straightening up the house and putting the toys where they belong is pretty much par for the course, and asking a nanny to do it doesn't usually provoke much prickliness. Problems crop up, though, when a caregiver's definition of neat differs from yours, in which case you have to weigh how important the housekeeping is against how good her childcare is. If she takes great care of the kids, it might be worth you while picking up some of the slack—and the toys—yourself.

Then there are errands like dry cleaning pickups, shoes from the repair shop, video returns, and post office runs—part of the daily grind. If the nanny can work any or all of these non kid-related errands into her day, fine. But you really shouldn't expect her to do too many of them. And don't try to pass off your own dirty work, like returning a piece of kids' clothing after you've thrown the tags out, unless the nanny absolutely doesn't mind. Plenty of bosses in the corporate workplace ask their assistants to run routine personal errands, and plenty of assistants resent it. If you sense reluctance on your nanny's part, don't push. The best tactic is to ask; you just never know what kinds of requests will press the wrong button, or which she'll do happily. A sitter may cheerfully drop off library books and gas up the car, but bristle when asked to water the plants.

Of course some nannies simply never say no. They do everything they're asked, do it well, and don't whine. Parents who are so lucky often end up throwing more and more chores at their sitters. This is the "good nanny" version of the "good child" syndrome, in which the better she is and the less fuss she makes, the more you expect of her—sometimes unrealistically. Be fair. That's the best way to keep someone happy—and keep her, period.

An Extra Load of Work

I've started to leave the laundry basket out, hoping my sitter will pitch in during her down time. She's ignoring my hints.

Unless you were very clear about what you expected when you hired her—that she wash, say, everyone's clothes plus the linens—then doing the laundry (other than the kids') is by no means a given. Some nannies are happy to help however they can. Others take the position of "I don't do windows," in which case you could always offer to pay her a little extra to make it worth her while. What's not fair is to expect the wash to get done in the fifteen minutes a sitter has free between preparing meals and cleaning up the kitchen. As for those hints, maybe she's not getting them because they're too subtle. Don't ask her to read your mind.

My friend asks her nanny to iron both her own and her husband's shirts rather than send the clothes out. This would be a huge help in our household, not to mention a big saving. But though our sitter probably has the time, I feel funny about asking her.

There are two kinds of ironing: the once-in-a-while favor (a kid's party dress) versus the daily grind. Asking a nanny to do the latter is like asking her to polish the silver. These "maidlike" tasks aren't usually expected of nannies and requesting them can cause friction, unless you've made them a requirement from the get-go. Every so often you'll meet that rare person who actually *likes* to iron, finding the task relaxing and satisfying. There's no harm in throwing the question out there, phrased in such a way that the sitter doesn't feel cornered. A simple, "How do you feel about ironing?" leaves room for a yay or nay.

Our nanny helps out with the wash, which I appreciate, but sometimes she's careless about reading labels. Last week she ruined an expensive "dry clean only" sweater. Shouldn't she make it up to me somehow?

It's out of line to ask her to fork over cash for the sweater—she's not a dry cleaner who gives guarantees for these things. She made a mistake and probably feels terrible about it. Of course you made a mistake too by throwing the sweater in the laundry to begin with. If her recklessness is consistent—she routinely mixes whites and darks—you have two choices: Take the laundry duty back or live with a little gray.

Overheard: The Home-cum-Laundromat

Our sitter had been cheerfully doing the family laundry for several months before it struck me that she was spending an inordinate amount of time in the basement. At some point I asked her if the work was too much, and she said, "No, not all." One day, while she was out with the kids, I went downstairs to pull something out of the dryer, and I discovered that nothing in the dryer belonged to me! I looked around and saw two duffel bags filled with the sitter's own clothes. I felt taken advantage of—I was essentially paying her to do her own laundry, and I was annoyed that she hadn't asked me. When I mentioned it, she answered defensively, "The laundromats in my neighborhood are closed by the time I get home. I thought you wouldn't mind." After I'd gotten over the initial surprise, I realized I didn't mind all that much, but I did ask her to come in a half an hour early or stay a little later on laundry days, and that suited her fine.

KEEPING ORDER

Our house is spotless since we hired our new sitter, but I can't help feel that she'd rather vacuum than get down on the floor to play a game with the kids. The other day, my youngest daughter was taking a nap and my three-year-old was playing alone, while the nanny was scrubbing the tub. Even though no one seemed unhappy, I felt she wasn't putting her focus in the right area.

This may be a simple case of the nanny working hard to please or impress the employer. But it's also possible she's using housework to escape the demands of childcare. After all, sweeping can be less taxing than interacting with a three-year-old and dealing with all her moods and demands. If, however, when you hired the sitter, you discussed her doing some housework, you may simply need to talk about the balance—when to do what: floors only once a week, bathrooms twice, and so on. Then, next time she picks up a mop, underscore your wish with a, "kids first, house second" kind of comment. You could also encourage long days out of the house by dropping them at the zoo or museum. Still, if you sense that no matter what, the caregiver doesn't seem genuinely interested in playing with the kids, it's time to look for someone who knows the meaning of light housework—and good childcare.

My nanny is wonderful with the children, but she's not the neatest person in the world. I've asked her to keep the apartment straightened up, but she just doesn't seem to have it in her.

Some people are born organizers; many simply aren't and don't even see a mess as a mess. It's the rare nanny who has an equal aptitude for, and interest in, childwork and housework. You hired her to be a babysitter, and if she's delivering on that score then you may need to give up on the idea of the house being as neat as a pin. Still, if the place is *really* out of control, and order is *really* important to you, then try being very explicit about where things go—from magazines to toys to mail to nail clippers. And be prepared to follow your own dictate, otherwise the best-laid organizational plan won't work. Another possibility: Your sitter can't control the chaos because you've got an overflow of kids' paraphernalia, not to mention stacks of magazines, catalogs, junk mail; maybe it's time for a little spring cleaning, no matter the time of year. A third, more challenging scenario is a nanny who stages a silent protest because she considers cleaning out of bounds. If that's the case, you're up against an attitude, and that's tough to change. You can deliver an ultimatum (keep things tidy or else . . .), which may be effective in the short term but will probably breed bitterness in the long run. Whatever solution you try, this kind of standoff often spells the beginning of the end.

It sounds petty but it drives me crazy: When I come home, I find the dishwasher full of clean dishes, which is great except that it's not emptied. I wish the sitter would finish what she starts.

You see it as not finishing a task; no doubt, she thinks she's doing you a favor by starting the job. Parents can often fall into the martyrish role of thinking that they're spending all this money on help but not getting what they need done—forgetting that what they hired a nanny for is childcare. Of course, if the half-baked scenario happens all the time (laundry half done, beds half made, dinner half started), you may have a nanny who is simply going through the motions and doesn't really take these jobs seriously. Since you do, you've got to come right out and ask her which chores she likes, which she abhors, and which, most importantly, she has time to see all the way through.

When I hired my part-time sitter for our infant daughter, I asked her if she'd mop the kitchen floor whenever she had the time. It's been three months and she's done it exactly twice. I frequently ask, "So did you mop the floor?" and she answers, in a perfectly cheerful way, "Oh, not today."

Chances are you were never comfortable asking her to mop the floors in the first place. Many parents have a way of asking passively—"If you have time, would you mind . . ." or "if you get around to it . . ."—that leaves a lot of room for misunderstanding. You need to be willing to say directly, "I really would like you to do the floors every day that you work." If you can't imagine yourself making such a request, grab the mop yourself.

Overheard: The Nanny as Neatnik

My Finish nanny was a neat freak. I started out being grateful, because ours isn't the easiest house to keep clean—we have four children between the ages of five and seventeen. We'd been through a string of sitters who could barely keep the playroom straightened, let alone the rest of the house together. So the return to order was welcome. But this nanny was so tidy, so finicky about the way the kitchen looked, that I was completely intimidated by her. I couldn't leave a dirty dish out or the newspaper sprawled on the table without getting disapproving looks. My husband and I decided to live with the "tyranny"—in part because we were thrilled to know where things were for a change, but also because it's hard to let go of someone who is so industrious and competent. Every few months I'd tell her to ease up—that it wasn't necessary to power-scrub mud off the soccer cleats or iron the underwear. But she couldn't help herself. I was reluctant to fire her, but after a year she'd had enough of our boisterous, messy family and she left us. It turned out she got out of the nanny field altogether. The last I heard, she'd opened her own pristine antique store, which probably suits her far better.

Wearing a Chef's Hat

My last sitter often cooked dinner for us and had it waiting on the stove when I got home from work. My new nanny shows no inclination to do any cooking aside from microwaving fish sticks.

You were lucky to be so spoiled before. There are few things more comforting than having a meal prepared for you; it taps into that feeling, childlike, of wanting someone to nurture you. The reality is that most nannies do a minimal amount of cooking, and do it mainly for the kids. Nannies who extend themselves are usually acting on their own initiative because they really love to cook and think nothing of turning out great big stews, chilis, or curry dishes; they're the type of cooks who don't consider being in the kitchen a burden. Hopefully, a nanny who can't or won't cook brings other interests and strengths to the table. Think of those the next time memories of your ex sitter-chef waft over you.

My nanny went to cooking school and used to work as a housekeeper-cook before she came to us. I also love to cook and I find there's a bit of competition going on in terms of who rules the kitchen and makes the best meals.

As the saying goes, too many cooks. . . . It's normal to feel territorial about someone who has moved into your domain. Ultimately you're the boss, but you don't want to pull rank to the point that you cut the nanny off from the kitchen (especially on those days, and they will come, when you're not able or in the mood to cook). Power struggles over turf, culinary or otherwise, usually find their rightful balance after a while. In the meantime, you could try carving up the week between you.

I appreciate the fact that the sitter cooks for the kids, but she has a limited repertoire, and what she makes is very bland. I'd like to expose the kids to a broader, healthier palate. If I don't say anything, she'll cook macaroni and cheese every night.

No one's ever suffered from a steady diet of pasta and, in fact, most little kids prefer the familiar anyway. But if you want to move the culinary experience up a notch, you're going to have to at least provide the raw materials (stock the kitchen with fresh vegetables, good cheeses, healthy grains, etc). And then, without criticizing her cooking, make specific suggestions about how to spice up the menus, telling the sitter that you want the kids to try as many different foods as possible. If your sitter's from another country, ask her to make some of her own favorite dishes from home. She may be simply cooking what she thinks American kids like and you may discover that she's got a whole other cooking style up her sleeve.

Overheard: The Non-Cook Cook

When I hired my caregiver, she was pretty explicit about not liking to cook. She said, good-naturedly, "I'd rather do anything else—cleaning, laundry, whatever." So, because I liked her, and I knew I'd have to compromise on something along the way, I said okay. I figured I could handle meals for a baby and a toddler. For the first few months, I'd cook the kids' dinner and then let the nanny do the feeding and cleaning up. As time went on, I'd simply put everything out—the pasta or the hamburger meat— and begin the process (put the water on to boil), leaving her to do the actual preparation. Little by little, without either of us discussing it, she was taking over the kids' mealtimes. It got so that we'd talk at some point during the day about what she could fix for dinner, and she'd go ahead and put the meal together, not seeming to mind at all. I realized that when she had said she hated to cook, she meant complicated, from-scratch dinners, which at this stage of our life are a rarity anyway. Most of the meals she made were simple—sometimes just reheated leftovers or frozen ravioli with jar sauce. Still, she took the job off my hands, and I'm happy to wait a few years for the children's gourmet experience.

ENDLESS ERRANDS

At least once a week it happens that I come home from work to find that we've run out of milk, and I have to turn around and go to the store. It irks me because usually I've just passed the deli on my way home.

Keeping track of milk and other kid staples like, cereal, lunch foods and juices typically falls under a nanny's jurisdiction. If it's not practical for her to get to the market because she doesn't drive or it's pouring rain, she should try to get in touch with you wherever you are—a minor interruption that could offset a bigger inconvenience when you get home. You could also instigate a morning routine of having her jot down a list of items that are running low (some parents tape to the fridge a list of household staples, from toilet paper to apple juice, to be checked off as supplies dwindle). Even if you're physically responsible for getting the goods, she carries the bigger burden of staying on top of everything.

Nanny Point of View: The Unstocked Fridge

"In my previous nanny jobs I was in charge of the grocery shopping, but in my new position I'm not. At first I was relieved to be off the hook, but I now find myself wishing the shopping were part of my job. The parents are busy and can't ever seem to get to the store to pick up what we're running out of. Or they forget things. I might mention that we need bread, but when the shopping is done, the bread is missing and I'm making the kids sandwiches out of crackers."

Last week I was totally work-crunched and I asked my sitter to help me out: I needed her to pick out a birthday present for my

six-year-old niece, and have it wrapped and mailed that day. I was surprised she was so grumpy about it.

She may find it somewhat demeaning to do your personal chores. Look at it from her perspective for a moment. She's a professional caregiver, not a personal shopper. If you ask for these kinds of errands frequently and get the same response, take the hint and don't ask anymore; you run the risk of making her unhappy with what is otherwise a good situation. But if this is an isolated incident (either your request or her reaction), it may be the manner in which you asked (or demanded) more than the fact of the errand itself. In any case, you should feel comfortable soliciting the occasional favor, and granting it, too—letting her borrow your car when she's moving apartments, mailing a package for her when you happen to be going to the post office. If you feel the give and take isn't there, think about how much you're each giving.

Nanny Point of View: The Errand Schlep

"I don't mind grocery shopping or dropping off the dry cleaning or returning videos, as long as the errands don't become overbearing. It's not fair to drag the kids all over town and in and out of the car. They're not getting anything out of the running around, and it's certainly not fun for anyone."

We've got this new sitter who has lots of energy and is eager to please—to a fault. Without my asking, she took a bag of mine to the shoemaker to fix a shoulder strap, she dropped off a roll of film that was sitting on the counter, and she used petty cash to buy a new cutlery organizer, then proceeded to rearrange our silverware drawer. It all feels a bit invasive.

This is the nanny-to-the-rescue phenomenon, in which a sitter swoops into an employer's house and life, and takes it upon herself to mend all the little frayed ends. The presumption may irritate, but don't read too much into the enthusiasm. As the sitter settles into the job and feels secure, odds are she'll ease up on the eager-beaver act. In the meantime, she's probably patting herself on the back for anticipating your needs, even if they're phantom ones (you were planning to give the bag away and the film happened to be overexposed). In the unlikely event that you sense she's trying to insinuate herself into the family structure in a way that's creepy, don't wait for the next shoe to drop—or be fixed—to cut her loose.

Overheard: Walking the Dog

Our sitter had been with us for a few years, with no complaints on either side. But last Christmas we gave the kids a puppy and it never occurred to me that having a dog would cause a problem. It turned out that the sitter had absolutely no interest in feeding or walking, let alone scooping up after him. She wouldn't even fill the water bowl. We talked about it a bit—I explained that if we were to continue with full-time help, she would need to pitch in with the dog duty. She nodded, but whether she was scared of our friendly Labrador or just felt the work was beyond the scope of her duties, I'm not sure. Finally, it got to the point where I would have to leave work in the middle of a meeting to go home and let the dog out the back door. We knew something had to change—and we knew we couldn't take the dog away—so we gave the nanny a choice: We'd help her get used to the dog, or else she'd have to leave. She decided to go.

Chapter 8

The Other Mother

Hiring a nanny is not just a business deal, it's a personal arrangement with an emotional subtext. And it's rife with paradox. We don't want someone to replace us as parents, but we want someone to come awfully close. The nanny should be nurturing, dependable, and spirited—someone who'll love our kids as her own. But—wait—aren't we paying her to love our kids? And isn't that too much to expect anyway? Being a nanny is a job, after all. And though plenty of caregivers do adore their charges, they have their own lives to think about and get back to at the end of the day.

While a nanny is at work, however, it's natural for her to assume the role of surrogate and take on many of the day-to-day childcare tasks. Someone has to make breakfast, pack lunches, and bathe the little ones—and if not one of the parents, who else? Nonetheless, a lot of parents grapple with guilt over letting the sitter read the baby to sleep or drive the kids back and forth to hockey practice. But the truth is, in time, they usually get (*very*) used to having the nanny do these deeds. Mothers, however, sometimes feel supplanted by nannies—new parents in particular may feel inadequate in the company of a skillful caregiver, or jealous of her bond with the baby. Feelings of guilt and jealousy normally pass as the parent comes to appreciate the third set of hands and realizes that, despite a loving nanny, the child is bonded to the parent for life.

On the other hand, delegating—even on the most practical, logistical level—doesn't come naturally to everyone. There are plenty of parents who are quick to admit they're loath to give up any control, as if doing so is tantamount to ceding some essential part of motherhood. Unable or unwilling to switch gears when they leave the house, they find themselves wondering throughout the day about the children and the nanny. They feel most comfortable calling all the shots, making all the arrangements; they even need to mastermind a schedule of activities for home. But the reality, especially for a working parent, is that you can drive yourself crazy trying to micromanage your child's and sitter's day. And for a caregiver, the loss of control can be demeaning and undermining of her authority.

On the flip side are those parents who leave in the morning, hand over the reigns and turn off the responsibility button. They get so swept along by their own, often chaotic days, that they tend to tune out the home front. It's amazing, in fact, how many of us haven't the foggiest idea where our children are spending whole afternoons. There's a fine line between delegating and abdicating responsibility. You want a caregiver to take the job and run with it—but not out of range, not too far. On a purely practical level, you don't want to be so oblivious that you wouldn't know where to look or call to track down your nanny if you needed to talk to her. And on another level, a parent who's out of touch with what's going on at home may end up feeling just that way, and may even begin to resent the caregiver or her own involvements outside the house.

One of the toughest roles a parent has to share is that of disciplinarian—a job that has less to do with duties per se than with attitudes. Do you approve, in theory, of time-outs? What about punishment by other means? Withholding a favorite toy? A promised play date? Almost everyone, even the novice parent, has basic ideas about how he or she wants their kids treated, and those ideas should be stated right at the beginning, on the first day, at the first meeting with the nanny. There's always room for adjusting the rules along the way; as specific incidents arise, they create forums for discussion about how to handle the next one.

Style is a key factor in how discipline is divvied up. Some parents are happy letting a nanny play the softy, while others would rather have a strict sitter who insists on good manners and certain rules—about not throwing food, say, or jumping on the bed—because they, the parents, are naturally laissez-faire. And everyone has a different threshold of tolerance for kids' tantrums, whining, and pouting—hopefully, the nanny's is pretty high.

In or Out of the Loop

The more I trust our nanny, the more I ask her to do the lion's share of the decision making about what the kids eat, who they play with, what kinds of activities they sign up for. The sense of liberation from planning is great, but I sometimes feel excluded from the inner circle.

There are bound to be times when parents wish they were more keyed in to the nitty-gritty childrearing stuff—from teaching the fine art of eating with a fork to dealing with the fine points of potty training. And there are just as many times when parents, once they have the control, are desperate to hand it over. The best nanny–employer relationships have ebbs and flows—the balance is just right, then off, then right again. No matter what, you never want to feel as if you can't step in and take over a childcare task that you'd like to do—after all, you are the parent.

I went away on a business trip for a few days and left my eleven-month-old with his regular caregiver. When I got home he was sitting on her lap. I went to pick him up to give him a hug and he immediately reached back to her. For a second it seemed he knew her better.

The parent–nanny dynamic is peppered with these kind of emotional tug-of-war moments, and working mothers with young babies are especially sensitive to bouts of nanny favoritism. It's easy to read too much into a natural occurence: The baby may simply have been in a groove with the nanny and you broke the mood; perhaps your entrance startled him and he instinctively turned to his "protector." How the nanny responded is more telling: Did she turn him back to face you or hold on to him? An important part of the nanny's job is to help nurture the primary parent–child relationship in whatever way she can—by talking up your homecoming if you've been away, and engaging you as "mommy" whenever you are there. If you don't feel you're getting this kind of support, and particularly if you feel displaced in your own home, you need to clear the air. In any case, try to look beyond your immediate feelings of jealousy and you'll realize that the kid's connection with the nanny is a good thing—it means he's getting lots of affection. And try to remember that while nannies are hired and fired, parents and kids are in it for the long haul. Children know who butters their bread.

Overheard: Who's First for the Firsts?

My husband and I went away for the weekend for a much-needed break, and left our one-year-old with her nanny. Wouldn't you know, while we were gone she took her first steps. The night we got to our hotel we called home, and the nanny told us it had been an exciting day—our daughter was on the verge of walking. The second night, we got the report that she'd taken a tentative try. By the time we were back home the next night, our daughter was cruising the coffee table pretty steadily. My initial reaction at hearing that the nanny saw that first step was jealousy: I'm the mom, and I should get to witness all the firsts— the first solid foods, the first day of school, the first lost tooth. My second reaction—later that night after a glass or two of wine—was, I will always see the first: When I'm with my daughter and she does something new, it will always be the first time for me.

THE ÜBER-NANNY

We're going through a nanny-is-God stage with our five-year-old son. Her grilled cheese sandwiches taste better than mine, and I don't even rinse the shampoo from his hair the "right way."

It's easy to feel put out when you're constantly being upstaged by a paid employee. But try to rise above it. You don't want to get into a tit-for-tat dynamic, you don't want to use your kids as pawns in a "best at" competition, and you certainly don't want the nanny to stop cooking her famous grilled cheeses or whatever else she does so well. Inevitably, she will slip from the pedestal anyway and suddenly it will be the best friend's mom who makes the world's greatest spaghetti. It's the nature of childhood: Kids are constantly falling in out and of love with key figures in their lives—teachers, best friends, siblings, caregivers. In the meantime, be thankful the kids are handing out nanny compliments rather than complaints, which are far harder to listen to and to handle.

I'm a new mother, and I appreciate how competent our nanny is with our six-month-old twins. But she's so knowledgeable and eager to take charge that I'm beginning to resent her and her experience.

At first, most new parents feel overwhelming gratitude for having the expert help on hand—especially with newborns, and especially with twins. But as you get your footing, it's only natural to bristle at being told what to do. Before you assume the nanny's being pushy and autocratic, make sure you're not being overly sensitive—you could be reacting out of your own insecurities. Step back and try to be objective: A nanny who's babysat for ten-plus kids has plenty to teach. Still, no amount of childcare experience matches a mother's instinct for nurturing her own children. Ideally, the two frames of reference—yours and hers—should complement rather than cancel each other out.

THE DAILY DETAILS

I'm pretty slapdash about giving my kids vitamins in the morning. I do it when I think about it, and if I don't have time, I leave the bottle out on the counter for the sitter. Occasionally we discover that neither of us has given the vitamins.

A lot of parents delegate by default—whoever more regularly takes on the task, whether it's unpacking a lunchbox or gathering up the yard toys, inherits the job. This kind of lackadaisical management style is fine—until it creates friction when something quasi-important doesn't get done. Besides, it can leave holes in a child's care. Be clear about responsibilities, as in: "I'll give the kids their vitamins each morning, but I'm turning the bath duty over to you." And be consistent; let the routine become just that. You'll spend less time thinking about the daily minutia—and in and of itself that constitutes freedom.

I have our au pair get the children dressed in the morning. The trouble is, her taste is wild (and wildly different from mine) and the kids leave the house in getups that make me flinch.

When your own children are discovering their sense of style, there's something endearing about watching the creative process. But when it's someone else's "bad" taste parading about, it's hard to see the charm. As lightweight as the topic of clothing seems, it can become an issue for those who have a strong aesthetic (even the way the nanny herself dresses can be an issue). If you can't really stand the way the kids look, lay out their clothes the night before. If you don't want to do that, or can't bring yourself to say anything, or the kids insist on the eclectic outfits, live with the situation. Remember, an au pair is only with you a short time—chances are she won't mark the children's sense of style for life.

Our three-year-old son loves to play in the bath, and the sitter will happily kneel beside the tub singing and playing for half an hour or more. I don't have such patience. When I bathe him on the weekends, I want to get him in and out in five minutes flat—and he resists.

It's inevitable that different people (including, for that matter, two parents) will have different thresholds of tolerance for daily "child maintenance." One person, for example, may have endless patience when it comes to doing puzzles—which is another person's idea of pure tedium; someone else may be able to push a swing for twenty minutes—a repetitive task that would drive you bananas. It's possible that your annoyance is fueled partly by jealousy or the feeling that the hired "parent" is naturally more suited to caring for kids. But before you dwell on your own incompetence, remember that the caregiver is getting paid to be patient. And whether she genuinely likes the bath task or is putting on a good show, who cares? Your kid is having fun.

I feel strongly about having my son get outside and get fresh air every day, short of a blizzard. My sitter, who's from the West Indies, hates the cold and is reluctant to go out when there's the least chill in the air. Since she's with him five out of seven days, I'm afraid she'll have more influence over whether he grows up liking the outdoors.

A lot of people from tropical climates have a hard time acclimatizing to colder zones—so if you look at the reluctance as a cultural difference, not as a sign of wimpiness or obstinance, it's easier to empathize. But that doesn't mean you should let a stay-at-home sitter completely off the hook, either. Anytime a parent has a strong feeling about how to bring up a child—in this case, emphasizing the value of fresh air and outdoors play—the parent holds sway. Insist on your principles, and insist she put on some extra layers and get out of the house. But be realistic and understanding about how far she'll want to go—which may be just a walk around the block, at least until spring.

My kids love to do their homework with the sitter before I get home, and I suspect it's because she's generous with help. She does the cutting for collages and looks up words in the dictionary, which I'd rather the kids did themselves.

Like many parents, she probably wants the children to do well, and sees their successes as a reflection of her own. In any case, you can't assume the nanny knows how you'd want her to handle the home-work issue—you need to go over the guidelines just as you would other house rules, such as TV time and snack policy. Vague advice (i.e. "just help the kids when they need it") isn't very useful. Be specific: Is she allowed to correct spelling or punctuation? Offer up the right answer? Take research materials out of the public library or search the Internet while the kids are at school? Or do you wish her to simply check whether the work is complete? Whatever the boundaries, remember, you've hired a nanny, not a tutor.

PLAY DATES AND PARTIES

My son has been invited to a weekday birthday party. I work full time, so I'd need to send the sitter in my place. I'm guessing she'll be one of the only non-parents there. Is there any protocol about this sort of thing?

There are two "parties" involved here: your nanny and the host. As for the sitter, there's no way of knowing how she'll feel if you don't ask. First off, don't assume that party duty would bother her. While some nannies feel ill at ease, or semi-servile, in a sea of parents who may exclude them from the conversation, others are able to hold their own or don't mind hanging back a bit. Host-parents, meanwhile, may have strong opinions on the sub-ject. Best to call and ask if there will be other caregivers present. If you get negative feedback all around, you could always ask another *parent* to take your child along with her kid. Or decline the invitation. Between the ages of three and six, birthday invites are a dime a dozen. Unless it's a best friend's birthday, the kids will forget. Your nanny may not.

Until recently, my young son often played with a good friend's kid, and the two nannies became buddies. Then the nannies had

a falling out—so the boys don't get together anymore. My husband and I are split over whether we should insist they keep their play dates.

As the parents/bosses you can, of course, insist. One could argue that the sitter's obligation to the child comes first and that interpersonal relationships between nannies shouldn't impinge on professional duties. Sitters are often thrown together in all kinds of playgroups and classes because of the kids—and that's part of the territory. (And in fact, two sets of parents may not be crazy about each other either but they'll still get together for the kids' sake.) But, realistically, there is a persuasive argument against forcing the issue: If the nannies genuinely don't get along, they're not going to interact well, and that may not be such a picnic for the kids.

My son is entering the play date age, and he's been having a lot of friends over. I don't know how much extra if anything, I'm expected to pay our sitter?

Most nannies say supervising playdates is all part of the job and they don't expect extra money for having another kid on their watch. That's assuming the kids are friends and there's reciprocity—your child gets invited to his buddy's house now and then, too, leaving your nanny a little free time. And if the other child's nanny comes along, too—often the case with little ones—then you certainly wouldn't pay more. It's another story, however, if your nanny feels she's being used for drop-in day care—a neighbor asks if she can "park" her kid (who happens to be three years younger than yours) at your house. In that case, a nanny really is doubling her workload and deserves compensation from the dumping parent. Evenings are a whole different kettle of fish. Almost all nannies expect to be paid extra—at least time-and-a-half—to watch additional kids.

Nanny Point of View: Hyperactive Scheduling

"My employer reads a lot of parenting books, and somehow she's gotten the idea that the more stimulation, the better. So she's scheduled a total of four days of activities for her seventeen-month-old son— gym class, music class, and swimming twice a week. I think the kid is overstimulated, and he gets grouchy every time we have to rush over to an activity. The next day he's tired and I'm having to push him out the door to yet another exciting class. I only wish my employer would see the value of one-on-one interaction with me, and creative exploration closer to home."

CALLING THE TIME-OUTS

My husband and I have been working with our daughter on controlling her temper, and now and then we give her a "time-out" to calm her down. The other morning, however, I heard the sitter do the same and it made me uncomfortable.

Most parents can justify their own or their spouses' disciplinary tactics, but they have a reflexive, protective response as soon as they hear another adult, even a relative, exhibit disapproval of any kind toward their children. If your nanny handled the situation in a kind, appropriate way, be thankful that she's taking an active role in trying to teach better behavior. If, on the other hand, you felt she had a nasty, out-of-proportion reaction (say your daughter threw her socks on the floor and wouldn't pick them up), it's time to define what you see as a punishable offense and make clear who does the punishing.

Sometimes when I give my three-year-old a time-out, he'll cry for a while, screaming, "I'm sorry! I'm sorry!" I try to ignore him so he really understands the lesson, but after a few minutes the nanny will go over to comfort him. I come off as the mean mom.

The nanny's move to nurture may be instinctual—she just can't help but console a crying child. A secondary motive may be as simple as her wanting a child to see her, the caregiver, as a protector and a source of solace. The end result, whether intentional or not, is that by interrupting your "lesson," she's negating the effect and undercutting your authority. If you're around each other a lot, you need to set up some ground rules about discipline: Namely, whoever starts a punishment should be able to see it through, and that includes *you* staying out of *her* way should she initiate disciplinary action. While you're hammering out the rules, make sure she understands your definition of a time-out— duration, place, and whether an apology is part of the reparation.

DIFFERENCES IN DISCIPLINE

Our nanny is even-tempered and soft-spoken, which I appreciate—except when it comes to discipline. My son loves to push his bowl off the high chair and take crayon to the walls. The sitter smiles weakly and says, "Please don't do that," and then proceeds to pick up the bowl and scrub the wall. I wish she'd get tougher.

The not-strict-enough sitter is a common complaint. Caregivers may do nothing in the face of bad behavior for fear that the children, or even the parents, won't "like" them (especially true with inexperienced nannies who aren't yet confident on the job). The downside of being too lax, of course, is that it can undermine your own efforts at discipline: You're trying to get your kids to make their beds in the morning, but the nanny does it for them when they forget (almost every day). Realistically, if the sitter is a softie by nature, she's not going to change into a taskmaster overnight. Still, it can't hurt to encourage her to reprimand when appropriate—with your blessing—explaining that it will help *you* in your endeavor.

I've noticed that our caregiver resorts to bribes a lot. She'll offer our daughter a sweet to clean up the room she's just demolished. It does work, but it's not a tactic I'm crazy about.

Parents, and nannies, tend to fall into two camps when it comes to bribes: Some endorse the idea that rewards encourage desirable behavior and that's what really counts; others strongly believe that if they give in (i.e., if you do this I'll give you that), they're not teaching true responsibility. But even those who take a high-and-mighty approach may find themselves offering the occasional present to mollify a child without thinking of it as a bribe at all—the promise to bring home a gift when they go off on a trip, for example. In any case, there needs to be a consistent policy—not only for the kid's sake, but for yours as well; if the nanny sets up a situation where the child asks and always receives, you end up looking bad. The solution may be to have the nanny shift the bribe from a monetary one to one that's more palatable to the parent, as in: "Once you clean up your room, we'll hang some of your artwork on the walls, not but until." For every iron-tight rule, of course, there's the inevitable loophole. There will be times that a bribe is allowed as a last resort. When the nanny finds herself in a terribly sticky situation with a screaming child standing on her head in the middle of a library, if she promises her a lollipop, well, there are worse things.

Nanny Point of View: The Big No

"I'm amazed by how little the kids I care for will listen to me. In my home country, Jamaica, when we say no to something, we mean no. Here, when I say no, the child screams back, 'You can't tell me what to do.' I've even heard, 'I'll report you to my Mom,' like I committed a crime. I let a lot of the discipline stuff slide because I don't want to lose my job, but I don't think I'm doing the children any favors by allowing them to be ill-mannered."

A friend of mine called to tell me she was shopping at the supermarket and saw our nanny screaming at our five-year-old daughter to put the gum back on the shelf. I was surprised that our sitter, who is typically calm and gentle in her admonishments, could show this other side.

One person's idea of verbal abuse may be another's definition of a raised voice. It's possible the nanny was simply speaking sternly and loudly—and that she'd already made her request sweetly, several times, to no avail. Since you weren't there, you need to ask for her version. As many parents know all too well, tantrums in stores can be hell to squelch. Before there's a next time, and you know there will be, come up with a strategy for public displays of temper—for example, pick up the screaming, kicking child and remove him from the scene as soon as possible. If your sitter has a loving relationship with your daughter, don't read too much into this one instance; if you're not convinced of that, the behavior she showed in the supermarket may be one reason why.

Overheard: Spoiled Rotten

I had my nanny take my two-year-old to the pediatrician for a routine physical. I asked her to ask the doctor to check for an ear infection, which I thought might be connected to all her tantrums of late. That afternoon the nanny called me at work to give me a rundown. She told me the doctor said our daughter had no ear infection, so we must be spoiling her. This prompted an incredibly tense conversation, during which I got defensive. The nanny started explaining what the doctor meant, using examples of things she'd observed, and it became clear as she went on that this was not the doctor's opinion, but hers. She brought up the fact that my husband and I let my daughter take CDs out of their cases and play with them. When I responded that we didn't mind so much because the discs are nearly indestructible, she went on to say she thought we weren't setting limits and that it would be better to explain to the child, "That's not a toy." By the time I got home I was really upset. I told the nanny that what I'd wanted to hear from the doctor was that the tantrums were normal, not, "You're doing something wrong." When she left that night, our conversation had gotten so uncomfortable, I wouldn't have been surprised if she didn't come back. The next morning, though, she arrived; I apologized and so did she. She explained that she was really just trying to be helpful. I said that the word "spoiled" had set me off—it was a loaded term for me. With a good night's sleep, I realized I'd overreacted, and that within the bigger context of our relationship, this was a very small event. The conversation cleared the air of any tensions that had been brewing for her around this area of discipline. She was able to tell me how much she loves the job, and I was able to tell her how much we value her. And, not least of all, it made it easier for us to talk openly about how we were going to deal—together—with the next tantrum.

We have a ten-year-old daughter who is the queen of the sassy remark. Apparently she offended the nanny by saying "you idiot" under her breath, and the nanny took it upon herself to forbid our daughter from having her next-door friend over, which seemed a bit drastic to me.

Perhaps because her feelings were hurt, she responded personally rather than professionally and went overboard. You probably can't control her reactions, but you can change the course of her actions, vis-à-vis your daughter. Draw up a list of which kinds of punishments suit what kinds of crimes, so nothing is decided in the heat of the moment. Some parents prefer to delay the sentencing until they can get home and do it themselves. If however, the nanny feels a situation warrants immediate restitution, ask her to call you at work or wherever you are so you can discuss what to do while it's happening. That way, she can punish by proxy.

IT'S NOON . . . DO YOU KNOW WHERE YOUR NANNY IS?

Our nanny likes to be out and about all day, and she takes our two kids on all kinds of adventures. I love the fact they're not housebound, but it makes it difficult to check in, because they're never home.

You may not be able to check in at home, but you can still check in. Agree on a certain time of day for a phone call—you to her, her to you, whatever works. If you happen to be out, she simply leaves a message that all is well and gives a quick update on plans for the rest of the day. If she knows she'll be unreachable at the agreed upon time, have her check in beforehand. To make the process smoother and more fool-proof, some parents buy their nannies beepers or cell phones—anyone who's ever been in a situation in which she needed to find the nanny and couldn't,

would probably agree that getting a sitter wired is a small invest-
ment for a secure sense of connection.

**My nanny asked if she could take my one-and-a-half-year-old
son on the subway to play with some of her cousin's kids in
Brooklyn, an hour from the city. I didn't want to seem distrust-
ful, so I said sure. Later, she told me that they had a great time,
but I felt I should have known more about where they'd be and
how to reach them.**

It's understandable that a parent wouldn't want a young child
traveling far from home—least of all to unfamiliar territory. So
why do many of us find ourselves nodding yes, when what we
really mean is no? Perhaps because we feel that by hesitating or
expressing doubt, we're showing a bias against certain neighbor-
hoods or raising the question of the nanny's competency. But
these niggling thoughts whatever their motivation are worth listening to. If you are the least bit unsure of your caregiver's sense
of responsibility—on the subway, in a crowded mall—restrict the
parameters within which they can venture, asking her to stick to
known entities. It's helpful for any parent (and especially a nervous or new one) to "see" the child at the playground or the
playmate's house—to be able to conjure a mental picture and
place him in a familiar frame.

**We've got a stay-at-home sitter who rarely ventures beyond our
own little neighborhood park. I make suggestions of different
places for her to take my daughter, but they go unheeded. I'd
love for her to be more outgoing—literally.**

It may well be that your suggestions are just that—an option that
can be opted out of. If she's a homebody, she will probably come
up with all kinds of semi-lame excuses—it looked like rain or it

was windy, or so-and-so was cranky and needed her nap. If you feel strongly about exposing your daughter to particular environments—libraries, nature trails, childrens' museums—make the excursion a requirement. You may have to officially sign your child up for a class or two so they have a time-and-place goal for several days a week—a solid reason to get out the door.

Overheard: Out of Touch

"I was out at lunch for an hour or so with a colleague, and when I came back to the office, the receptionist said my sitter had called several times. She rarely calls, so I was afraid something was wrong. As soon as the sitter answered the phone I blurted out, "What happened?" and she immediately assured me that the kids were fine, but told me that her husband had been in a terrible car accident and she needed to go to the hospital. She had gone through a harrowing hour before she was able to reach me, during which time she tried to call my parents (who were out of town) and the neighbors (who weren't home). She wouldn't, and thankfully didn't, abandon our kids, even though her personal life was hanging in the balance. Her husband recovered quickly, but I learned a critical lesson: Though I think of myself as reachable during the day, I'm obviously not always. In fact, even I were to give my nanny an hourly schedule of my whereabouts, I'd be bound to break it once in a while to do something spontaneous, whether it's going shopping for a birthday present or getting a spur-of-the-moment haircut. Now I always carry a cell phone when I'm out to lunch, or out to dinner, or, for that matter, just getting from one place to another during the day—which in and of itself can take me out of circulation for hours at a time.

A QUICK STUDY: COMMUNICATION CENTRAL

Beyond the ordinary, ever-useful phone call, families have come up with several successful strategies for keeping in touch with their sitters—both literally (to know who's where) and also emotionally (to feel connected).

The House Book Think of this as home station. An address book or old Filofax that's placed by the phone and filled with key phone numbers—play dates' homes, doctors' offices, health insurance ID info, superintendent's beeper, neighbors' homes and offices, as well as the less obvious but useful numbers such as the dry cleaners, video store, and pizza delivery. The nanny can feel free to add her own notations—of places she and the kids frequent, or new venues they discover, as well as the numbers of her friends and family who you may need to reach occasionally.

The Calendar Sounds obvious, but a large wall calendar or oversize desk book can streamline who does what for a day or an entire week, and pretty much erase the risk that one of you will assume the other is doing karate class duty or car pool. Nannies usually appreciate the clarity of having something on paper, rather than having to remember the slew of directions you unload as you leave in the morning. Some parents color-code the activities and errands—the nanny's in red, say, and theirs in black—or star what the nanny's responsibilities are, whether it's going to the grocery store, bathing kids, or making dinner.

The Journal This is both practical and sentimental—a forum for the nanny to record daily events and keep track of a child's emerging or disappearing habits, from nap times to bouts of crankiness to giving up the thumb, and, for older kids, friendship spats or favorite cookie recipes. The journal also affords a place for anecdotes, stories, and milestones, which places added value on the nanny's insights and input.

Chapter 9

The Good Boss

Even if you're a boss out there in the workplace, with a single assistant or a whole staff, you could well be on unfamiliar territory
when it comes to employing someone on home turf. How you approach the situation—with relish or trepidation—depends to some
degree on what you're used to. Those who grew up with help around
the house may slide right into the role of employer, unless they're
reacting against that upbringing. Those who didn't have a nanny
or housekeeper may find the boss role unnatural, even awkward, in
which case they've just got to learn on the job as they go along.

The best way to get comfortable with the hierarchical
employer–employee setup is to acknowledge and work with your
own personality. Naturally authoritative people are going to be
that way regardless; they have no problem giving orders, being
commander of the ship. Shy or insecure types tend to be instinctively solicitous, almost subservient, toward the employee. This
kind of boss will often beseech the nanny to do something, as if
asking for a favor. She might say, for example, "Do you mind
picking Max up from school today?" when what she really means
is, "Please pick Max up from school today"—not that one way is
better, but each carries a message. The first style implies that the

boss and sitter are partners, in it together; the second style rein-forces the relative status of the sitter.

Ultimately, as in any other job, the chemistry between em-ployer and employee is what makes the deal work or not. You're not operating in a vacuum. What she brings to the table in terms of attitude counts, too, and helps determine how the balance of power shakes out. One nanny may prefer the passive role, waiting for instruction, while another is confident, take-charge, and wants to be master of the house.

What's key across the board is respect for the sitter, and for the fact that she has a life outside of the job. And remind yourself what that job is, because it's easy—really easy—to start taking the nanny's work for granted. You should also respect a nanny for the sake of good relations—to keep her on the job. Parents who are on their third or fourth nanny in a year might simply be unlucky, but it's just as likely there's something about their atti-tude that needs adjustment. This type of employer often turns out to be someone who makes a nanny feel inept and under-appreciated, leading to increasingly poor job performance, and eventually to her quitting or being fired. In some cases, an ill-mannered boss just can't hold his or her temper, or may actually enjoy the drama of a confrontation.

Even the most even-keeled employer is bound to lose his or her cool once in a while. And that's not a deal-breaker, necessarily. A good boss knows how to apologize, or can later explain, calmly, the reason for the blowup. And if an employee flies off the handle, and is able to apologize and explain, the employer should be able to accept and move on. What's probably the toughest part of being a boss isn't getting over the occasional friction or fight, but know-ing how to talk—and criticize—constructively. General rule of thumb: Don't expect someone to read your mind. If you want the sitter to spend more time on the floor playing and reading with your child, tell her. Nicely. How you talk to a nanny is crucial in establishing the tenor of the relationship.

No matter what, a good boss is able to put herself in the sitter's shoes. If you work for someone yourself, use your own job as a paradigm. What makes the relationship with a boss, or an underling, smooth or thorny? What keeps you—or them—satisfied, gives you incentive? And even if you're not an employee yourself, you know on a gut level what inspires loyalty and respect.

THE BALANCE OF POWER

I didn't grow up with a nanny or even a housecleaner. But now that I have a child—and a job I want to go back to—I'm considering a full-time caregiver. Still, I can't get used to the idea of help in the house.

Think of caregiving as a profession, not as servitude. Assuming you pay a competitive wage, there's no reason to feel conflicted about providing someone with a good job. Anyway, times have changed and so have the associations with in-house help, especially with the two-working-parent phenomenon. These days, having a full-time babysitter isn't as much of a class statement as it used to be, although it's still the most costly form of childcare. As for emotional resistance to the notion of bossing someone, don't go against your nature. If you don't feel comfortable with a strict hierarchical arrangement, no one says you can't be democratic about it and try to establish a more informal working relationship.

My sitter has a habit of telling me what she thinks I ought to do about everything, announcing that the baby needs new shoes, or that we've got to do a big grocery shop today. Not that I mind her initiative, but her outspokeness makes me feel like she's running the show.

While it's nice to have a nanny who's on top of the household and cares enough to keep track of what needs doing, it can be unnerving to feel your control is being wrested away. It's a case of who's bossing whom. What's more, some parents will interpret a nanny's suggestions—rightly or wrongly—as veiled judgments on how well the parent is doing *her* job. On the other hand, a lot of nannies simply pride themselves on running a household— and very energetic types thrive on assuming responsibilities. Unless your nanny's being overly aggressive, then allow her room to have opinions and voice them—whether you take them to heart is another story.

Overheard: The Takeover

A year ago, I hired an amazing nanny—a woman who swept into our house, put everything in order, and took complete and effective charge of the kids, and as it turned out, of me, too. Since I work at home, she'd whip up soup and a salad using whatever leftovers she could find, set the table, and announce that lunch was served. At first I felt totally pampered, but after a week or so I began to resent having to be polite and eat whatever she made, and even having to take the break at all; sometimes I simply wanted to eat a cheese sandwich at my desk. The routine put me in a terribly awkward position. Not only was I uncomfortable being waited on (especially since I didn't hire her to do that), but I felt less in control of my house, and of her. Before I could figure out what to do, she unexpectedly quit and took a better-paying job with another family, a job in which she would be managing a large household. Obviously, the new position was more up her alley. Once I got over the hurt at being dumped, I realized I was relieved at having my house, and my routines, back to myself. And I was determined that the next nanny would be less domineering, if a little less can-do.

PEER PRESSURE

The very thing that attracted me to our nanny in the first place—
she's bright, educated, and happens to be from my hometown, San
Francisco—has now become a stumbling block to my being able
to be her boss. In another context, she might well be a friend.

But this is a different context and she accepted the job knowing she
would be an employee, not a colleague. There are all kinds of em-
ployer/employee relationships, so don't get hung up on the idea that
a boss has to be bossy; plenty of employers become social friends
with their underlings and when it works, it's great because it's fun
to be around each other, pure and simple. The other up side to this
dynamic is that the more similar the two of you are the more you
can trust her to "be you" in your absence and take care of your kid
the way you would. So you can be friendly, you can even be friends,
but you don't have to relinquish the real decision-making power of
a parent when it comes to important areas like discipline or education. In the end, the biggest risk of getting too cozy is the awkwardness of having to terminate the job, and, should that come to
pass, maybe the personal relationship, too.

A MATTER OF FORMALITY

No matter how many times I've reiterated to our caregiver that
she needn't call me Mrs. So-and-so, but please to use my first
name, she continues with the formal greeting.

The honorific may put you in an unfamiliar position of authority—it makes you think back to teachers and your parents'
friends. Maybe it seems old-fashioned, or simply makes you feel
old. Regardless, if you keep asking the sitter to change her ways
and it's not happening, you may be up against an ingrained sense
of etiquette—and that may be tough to undo. If she's used to

having the professional lines clearly delineated, it becomes a question of who's more uncomfortable, you or her? Assuming you can live with her style, why press her into an awkward position.

Overheard: Making Assumptions

In the past, whenever I've seen a well-dressed white woman walking along with a black nanny pushing a stroller, I've had the knee-jerk liberal response of feeling that the scene smacks of classism and racism. Why couldn't the mother, who I assumed had no pressing workload, be pushing her own child? Now I find myself on the other side of the looking glass, often walking down the street with a nanny pushing my child in a stroller. Who knows how many are judging me the same way? What they don't know—and what I didn't know then—is that the scene does not necessarily mean what you think. In my case, I'll sometimes take my two-year-old and nanny with me in town to stroll about while I run a couple of errands, or I'll accompany them on their way to the park because my daughter has insisted on showing me her new trick on the slide. And for all my worries about employing a "servant." My sitter and I have a very easy relationship—we know our roles but we also genuinely enjoy each other's company.

THE SKILLED CRITIC

There are a couple of things I'd like to straighten out with my nanny, like how she gives me phone messages a day late, and leaves toys lying about in the kitchen. But I'm afraid to say anything—I don't want to rock the boat.

Even those who command whole departments in corporate settings can lose the will to be authoritative when the conflict is

played out at home. The fear that the nanny will bolt if repri-
manded is one factor, the fear of retribution is another—someone
who is yelled at or put on the defensive may begin to harbor
resentment, and may even take out her feelings on your kids by
ignoring them or being irritable or impatient. Those parents who
feel particularly inept at handing down admonishments can and
should make a conscious decision to "practice" correcting the
sitter on small issues, like how to fold the towels (i.e. "I'm a little
finicky about how these stack up—let me show you how I fold
them"), just to get in the habit of having a friendly, non-charged
discussion. That way, when the big stuff comes up, the sitter is
less likely to jump into a defensive position.

**The sitter is often late—by about ten minutes, which throws
my entire morning off. She always has a good excuse, like she
just missed the train. I've said a few times that I can't be late
for my job, but I can't seem to get my point across.**

She may be hearing you, but the message is clearly not sinking
in. And that may have to do with the way you're soft-pedaling
the request in a casual, chit-chatty manner that belies how important you really consider punctuality. For her part, she could
be bad at figuring out how long it really takes her to make all the
commuting connections (some people are overly optimistic about
travel time and assume the light will always be green), in which
case she should at least acknowledge, and apologize for, her late-
ness. There are two employer techniques to get her to you on
time. The simplest is to request that she come fifteen minutes
early—at eight forty-five rather than nine o'clock—so if she's a
little late you have a cushion. If she's still not punctual, you have
to come up with a consequence—for example, make her next
raise contingent on being prompt. Though not the most pleasant
of routes, it's certainly an effective one.

Every time I express any disappointment in the way the nanny has handled something, she gets this wounded look. It makes it hard to have a constructive dialogue.

Either she's very sensitive to criticism in general, or your manner of communicating disapproval comes across as a put-down. The key to criticizing is style—less confrontational, more conversational. It's possible that when you're talking to her, you're making statements and declarations ("you never do this right" or "you always do that wrong") that don't allow for a response or open the door for an interchange. Engage her as much as you can: For example, if you're upset that she's letting the kids have way too many sugary snacks, rather than come down on her with a "I told you before" invective, propose a different approach, as in, "Why don't we try to limit junky snacks to once a day, and if they're still begging, we'll put our heads together and come up with a new tactic." This makes her part of the solution, not the problem.

Losing Your Cool

The other evening, after a bad day at work, I came home only to find out that the sitter never made it to the grocery store. I lost my temper and lit into her. She started to cry but, unmoved, I continued my diatribe. Today, of course, I'm not angry anymore and I'm not sure how to make amends.

It happens to the best of us, that carry-over from one arena (work) to another (home). The fact that the nanny happens to be there when you walk in means she may bear the brunt of a sour mood or become the perfect scapegoat for misplaced frustrations. An oversight on her part may be the proverbial straw that breaks the camel's back. And then if you're like a lot of remorseful parents you spend the next day going out of your way to be nice and solicitous, to the point where the offending behavior is glossed over. The trick is to say you're sorry—a simple apology does wonders in soothing battered egos. But impress upon her that there was a message behind the madness.

R-E-S-P-E-C-T

The other day I overheard my husband admonishing our sitter for not folding his khakis on the crease. Later, a friend of mine told me that our sitter told *her* sitter that she was upset by the scolding, saying "It's not even part of my job—I was just trying to help."

Remembering where a job begins and ends is a large part of being a sensitive boss. It's one thing to correct a caregiver on her caregiving technique; it's quite another to come down on her for something that's not even in her realm of responsibility. When a person makes a helping gesture, it's meant to be taken as just that—and when that gesture gets slammed, the giver is going to feel resentful. It's as if someone gave you a present and you responded by saying, "Thanks, but it's really not me." Hardly polite.

Nanny Point of View: I Have a Life, Too

"My boss asked me to come in Saturday in the middle of the day for an hour while she went to get her hair cut. It takes me at least half an hour to get to her house, so how could she think it would be worth my time on my day off? I felt like I couldn't say no, because she's my boss, but it made me feel she had no respect for my time off and the fact that I have a life outside the job."

I've finally got a nanny I like, and I don't want to lose her. But with my track record—four nannies have quit on me in the last two years—I'm concerned that I'm impossible to work for.

We could be talking a streak of bad luck and bad chemistry. Since so much of the success of an employer–employee click is personality-based, there's a lot of room for mismatches. But it wouldn't hurt to get a little introspective. Has there been any pattern in the way the nannies have quit or the things they've quit over? Did they leave following a dressing-down or after you turned down a request, for a day off, a raise, whatever? Did they all quit without the safety net of another job that you know of? If the answer is yes to any or all, chances are your nannies have been so unhappy—with the workload or with you—that they wanted out. One of the main reasons nannies get dispirited on the job and eventually disengage from the family is that they feel a lack of respect. Some employers, perhaps without realizing it, are condescending and dismissive of their employees—often in a misguided attempt to bolster up their "boss posture." Once they feel secure in their position of authority, they often ease up a little on their aggressive stance—and on their employees.

Overheard: Praise the Nanny

The other day I took my six-month-old son to the pediatrician for his first big checkup since our sitter started working for us. I came home and told her that everything was great, that my son got a stellar report. I went on about how much weight he'd gained, how much he'd grown, and other details about his progress. After a pause, she asked, "So what did the doctor say about how well he was being cared for?" I realized that I'd been going on about the visit but hadn't taken into account the fact that the nanny saw the checkup as a reflection on her. The truth was, she was doing a wonderful job, as I was quick to tell her. From then on, I took care to give praise and to remember that a nanny needs reinforcement, just like anybody on any job.

Part IV

Crimes and Misdemeanors

Chapter 10

Touchy Situations

Inevitably, they're going to come up—embarrassing or difficult situations that can lead to uncomfortable talks and, sometimes, to unpleasant resolutions. The trip wire can be a simple difference of opinion (not always so simple), or a violation of trust that goes deeper than the deed, or a crime—of property or of the heart.

As far as incendiary issues go, politics and religion rank right up there, particularly if both parties (nanny and employer) are outspoken or deeply fervent about their views. An agnostic parent, for example, may have a problem with a nanny who crosses herself all day long. A liberal may be aggravated by someone who's pro guns. And a Mormon nanny may be offended by a family that likes its cocktails. Personal differences, however, don't have to sabotage a relationship—as long as the children aren't dragged into the arguments and don't become pawns in a tug of war of ideals.

A more subtle, more insidious kind of destructive force comes in the form of sexuality or its corollary, jealousy. It's not unheard of, for instance, for a mother to become unhinged by a young sitter's good looks or her too-perfect body. She can also come undone by an imagined or real flirtation between the husband

and nanny. The possibility of a sexual come-on, from any quarter, is always present in a world of grown-ups. Regardless of whether anything actually occurs, the suspicions may be undermining enough of the mother-sitter relationship to warrant a change of face. It's not uncommon, either, for a mother to feel threatened by a competent, charming nanny—one who can "do everything": cook, clean, and sing, with one kid on her hip and the other happily playing at her feet; a woman who has the whole household under her spell. While occasional feelings of insecurity or competitiveness are normal in the parent–caregiver relationship, ongoing ones are rarely productive in the long run.

Minor crimes, like racking up long-distance phone calls or Internet charges, are obviously going to create some tension in the house and shake your faith in the nanny a bit. With these sorts of cases, parents aren't so much put out by the money factor but by a more general feeling that they're being taken advantage of. And usually they can shrug it off. If the transgression is more serious—a large wad of money or some jewelry is missing from its usual place in the dresser—it should be dealt with directly, as difficult as that may be for the nonconfrontational type. Otherwise, the suspicion, which may not be grounded in the first place, will fester and perhaps ruin a perfectly good relationship.

Deception in general—the feeling that something is going on behind your back—can wreak havoc on any relationship. Even if the offense seems harmless on the surface, it's almost always disturbing on a deeper level. Say you discover that the caregiver hangs out in your bedroom to watch videos while you're away (a neighbor happens to stop by and see), or she riffles through your desk drawers (though nothing's taken, things are never exactly as you'd left them). This kind of behavior can easily erode your confidence in someone you've engaged to work in the intimate environment of the home. A nanny, after all, is privy to a lot of inside information in terms of the house and its inhabitants. One of the most egregious betrayals is a breach of confidence about family matters to the outside world—divulging financial details or private medical conditions, for example, to a friend's nanny or a neighbor. Apology or no, confession or no, there's one indisputable rule in this business: You don't need a permit to fire someone. No one's looking over your shoulder, and you don't have to explain yourself to the world.

SEX AND POLITICS

We have a sitter who is young, blonde, and gorgeous. She's great with the kids, and they're crazy about her. Nothing's wrong with the situation except me—I feel frumpy and middle-aged in her presence.

She can't help her good looks or her youth, and assuming her behavior is totally professional, the problem (or paranoia) lies with you. Even so, your reaction is hardly out of the ordinary given the innate closeness of the parent–nanny relationship. It's not unnatural for a parent to get jealous, competitive, or angry—to experience the whole spectrum of emotions she might feel toward anyone under the same roof. But ultimately no one wants to feel uncomfortable in her own home, and some women admit they avoid the problem, consciously or not, by hiring nannies who aren't threatening and may very well be a little frumpy themselves.

Our nanny recently told me that my husband has been coming on to her in not-so-subtle ways, which I have a lot of trouble believing. I don't know what to make of it, or her.

The most benign possibility is that there's been a communication lapse. If your nanny's English is not crackerjack, perhaps she misunderstood a comment he made about, say, making the bed. Even if your husband is a notorious (albeit harmless) flirt, that doesn't necessarily excuse his behavior in this situation—if you want to keep your sitter, he's got to keep his tongue, among other things, to himself. There's always the unsavory possibility that he actually has been coming on to the nanny in a threatening or abusive way. In that case, legal problems are just the start of your troubles. As to whether you believe her (or him), that depends on your overall relationship with her (or him): Would she have reason to fabricate? What is she asking for? An apology? A way out? A payoff? Or is she simply meddling to cause trouble? We've heard some mothers wonder out loud about who's more irreplaceable— and in the case of a wonderful nanny (and lousy husband) fan-tasize about keeping the former and jettisoning the latter.

Nanny Point of View: A Show of Bias

"I'm uncomfortable being in the room when my em-ployer is watching the local news. Any time there's a story about a shooting or drug raid in the Bronx, she'll turn to me and say, 'Is that near where you live?' Even though I tell her no, I get the feeling she's lumped me in with a certain kind of dangerous neighborhood. How could she possibly know? She's never even asked me about my street, my building, anything, let alone seen where I'm raising my kids."

Ever since our leggy Finnish au pair arrived, my husband has been careening and preening around. I don't feel threatened, but I'm beginning to resent her presence, not to mention the length of her legs.

It's not unheard of, or even unusual, for au pairs to become objects of desire—they're young and their stay, (typically one year) has a definite end in sight. A flirtation or even an affair can be ap-pealing. To both parties. There are stories, of au pairs who carried on affairs right under the wife's nose and busted up a marriage. But whether the au pair is being provactive or not, if the household dynamic makes you uncomfortable, you have recourse. Transfers have been arranged by agencies for even mildly suggestive behavior.

I noticed the other day that my sitter has put a pro-life bumper sticker on her car. My husband and I are pro-choice, and while I don't mind if she has a different point of view, I don't want her proselytizing to my eleven-year-old.

Grown-ups should be able to handle their political differences, but add a child—an impressionable pre-adolescent, no less—to the picture, and things get more complicated, especially when the issue on the table is a political hot potato like abortion or gun control. You can't ask the nanny to remove her bumper sticker or change her personal beliefs but you can certainly ask her to keep her views to herself. Of course, if each time the sitter's car pulls into the driveway, you see her as the opposition, that's not a healthy situation. You may have to dissolve the relationship due to "irreconcilable differences."

Our new sitter is a devout vegetarian, and after three weeks my three daughters, ages four, six, and twelve, announced that they were giving up meat. I'm a little surprised by how much clout she has.

The good news is that your kids obviously respect and admire the babysitter—and they may simply be trying to win points with her by imitation. The mixed news is that she may be unwittingly exerting excess influence through her comments or reactions when it comes to meat. If she shrieks in disgust when she unloads some lamb chops from the grocery bag or has a running monologue about the ills of pork while you're making a ham sandwich, then clearly she's swaying the room. Any concern about your kids' diets may not even be germane if you feel that the sitter's power has eclipsed your own. For consolation, you can pretty much bet on the fact that the pendulum, as always, will swing back. Kids, fickle by nature, may well become avid carnivores tomorrow.

Overheard: Nanny at the Altar

We're not a religious family—and we've decided to raise our children without organized religion in their lives. My first clue that our live-in nanny felt differently about the importance of worship came on the day I heard church music coming from her room—really loud, really insistent hymns that were hard to ignore, although I tried. A few days later I was having dinner alone with the children, and they bowed their heads in grace before eating. We never say grace; this was obviously something they picked up from the new nanny. I let that go, too—for the moment. Another week or so went by, and then one day my five-year-old looked out the window and said, "Let us thank the Lord for all the beautiful flowers." But what finally forced a conversation between the nanny and me was her asking for a small table to use as a base for an altar to Christ. Once we started talking, it was clear she felt uncomfortable, too—about expressing her beliefs in a home that was devoid of faith. We came to a compromise: What she did in her room—the music, the altar—was her business. But what she did and discussed with the children was ours. No grace, no prayers, no preaching. It's been several years, and the peace has held.

DICEY VICES

We went out last Saturday night and came home to find our live-in sipping a glass of wine and watching the news. I'm not crazy about the idea of her drinking, although she didn't seem looped. I wonder if it's fair to hold her to a higher standard than we hold ourselves to?

Even though you may think nothing of having a few cocktails while you're home and "on duty," a nanny's drinking is a slightly different story. You know your tolerance; you don't know hers—it's possible one glass of wine might impair her judgment. And since she's working for you as a paid employee, her behavior translates as "drinking on the job"—not acceptable in almost any industry or workplace. But no one wants to play moral majority or mother to the sitter, which might be why this situation brings up conflicted feelings: Though you don't want her drinking, you can easily put yourself in her shoes (you might want to unwind on a Saturday night, too). The key is the timing: Make it clear that she can do what she likes when she's not on the clock.

I came home tipsy the other night after having a few drinks with some girlfriends. I remember babbling a lot to our sitter and remarking upon the amazing fact that there were suddenly two goldfish in the bowl. She shook her head and assured me there was still only one. I'm afraid she lost a little respect for me.

The more hierarchical the parent–caregiver relationship, the less room there is for mistakes or "bad" behavior on either side. Each is expecting the other to perform at her best all the time, which is an impossible standard to adhere to. Okay, so she saw a chink in the armor. Trying to dance around the issue only serves to legitimize it as a real concern; better to bring it up—and laugh it off. If you sense that the nanny can't laugh with you, then you may have a moral clash. You don't want to be in a position where you have to defend yourself to your nanny; nor do you want to start hiding your normal, healthy indulgences. It's on your shoulders either to correct her assumption or to challenge her presumption that she can be jury and judge.

Our daughter has asthma, and it was a job requirement that the sitter not smoke—but I smell nicotine on her clothes and worry she's lighting up on the job.

If your nanny's lying, that's a blow to your relationship right there. And where there's smoke there may be fire: She might not be taking your daughter's health problems seriously. But give her a chance to explain before you accuse. Could be, she lives with a smoker and her clothes carry the odor. It's also possible that she does smoke, but only on her way to or from work; in that case, you have to decide whether you're opposed to having a nanny who smokes at all, even on her own time, or can accept it—out of sight, out of mind. But if she satisfies her habit—and justifies it—by stepping outside your house to smoke while she's on the job, then she's taking a risk by leaving your child unattended. In any case, once your trust is breached, you risk a domino effect: You may well begin doubting her about everything.

I recently opened up our live-in's medicine chest in a mad search for aspirin and was surprised to see quite a lineup of prescription medication. Either she's got a drug addiction or a serious health problem, and both possibilities make me nervous.

Before you jump to conclusions, come straight out and tell her what you found. Start by saying you're concerned about her, and—remaining sensitive to a potentially embarrassing situation—ask her if there's a medical issue you should know about. The best-case scenario is that she's got a minor condition that's completely under control—one she felt was so minor, she didn't need to reveal it. And if you've never noticed anything unusual in her behavior, even on reflection, then her explanation should satisfy you. But a more serious illness or condition demands that you find out as many details as possible and even, with her permission, speak to her doctor about potential side effects or repercussions if she misses a dose. As for psychological illnesses such as depression or anxiety, they're going to set off alarms with most parents. But before you panic, get the whole story; medication may allow her to function fully. It goes without saying that if you suspect or discover that she's covering up a serious problem like an amphetamine addiction, it's time to put the lid on the relationship.

Petty Theft

I leave my sitter ample cash for milk, taxis, and incidentals, and I've never asked for any accounting. But lately it feels like there's less and less change left in the envelope.

A lot of parents play loosey-goosey with petty cash. They don't want to be, well, petty and start counting pennies. Besides, many are simply too busy to sweat it; they figure an extra five dollars here or there doesn't add up to much in the big picture. The only way to really keep track is to ask the nanny to hold on to receipts. Most parents put a small amount of cash—say twenty or thirty dollars—in an envelope and ask her to put the change back, along with the receipts and a notation of what was bought. Nannies generally are used to this accounting system and don't think twice about it. And for parents it can provide insights: You may find out that the sitter is indulging herself or your child with sweets, treats, inexpensive toys; if you wouldn't spend money on these things yourself, you may prefer that she didn't either.

Every Friday afternoon I go to the bank machine to withdraw cash to pay our sitter. This week, she called as soon as she got home to tell me that her salary was a hundred dollars short. I had the receipt from the machine and could swear I'd given her the entire wad. It flashed through my mind that she was lying.

Suspicion is an unpleasant feeling at best. If you trust her instinctively and have had no reason to doubt her integrity before, then you have to assume that even though you're sure you remember giving her all the cash, you miscounted or dropped a few bills. (Anyway, even if this were a desperate ploy for a little extra money, there's little chance someone would try it again.) If you have a habit of misplacing things, then you're the prime suspect. Pay her the money and chalk it up to a mysterious disappearance.

Overheard: Caught Shoplifting

About a month ago, I got a call at work from the police in our district. Our nanny had been arrested for shoplifting at the grocery store, and our three-year-old daughter was down at the station house with her. It turned out the store didn't press charges; they just asked our sitter to pay back the forty dollars she stole in groceries. By the time I rushed home, the sitter had been released and our daughter was happily playing at home on the kitchen floor, seemingly oblivious to the whole event. The nanny was extremely remorseful. She said she'd never stolen before, but that she was desperate and needed food for her family. We felt torn—she'd always been completely trustworthy, yet *she did break the law. Ultimately, we decided to give her a second chance. We allowed her to borrow $200 for a month to get her through this tough time, and in exchange she promised she would never, ever put our child in that kind of situation. But we couldn't follow through on our good intentions. Every time the phone rang at work I'd jump, sure she'd been arrested again. And each night we'd grill our daughter about how the two of them spent their day. In the end, we just couldn't get over it. We let her keep the loan—and we let her go.*

Stepping on Toes

Our live-in has a best friend who works as a daytime nanny in the neighborhood. The two are almost inseparable: The friend comes over when she gets off work and hangs out while our sitter feeds the kids dinner, and she shows up every weekend, too. It's getting to be a bit much.

Drawing social boundaries is especially tricky with live-ins, who need to have a life despite the fact that they're boarding in someone else's home. Before you bark too loudly and ban the buddy from the house, step back and assess. The issue to address is whether the sidekick is keeping your nanny from focusing on her job. Are the two sitters yakking when your kids are just zoning out in the front of the TV? If so, you're justified in limiting the visits. Or are they all playing together? If the situation works for the nannies, the kids—everyone but you—then you may just have to find your own refuge.

My sitter occasionally asks if she can bring her two-and-a-half-year-old son over to play with our son, who is only three months younger. The boys are pals, but there are times I sense she's doing it for her own reasons, and I don't want to be her child-care solution.

You may be—but that doesn't necessarily mean it's a bad situation, considering the kids get a play date out of it. If you're uncomfortable about the nanny's ability to handle what may be a handful, make a point of sticking around a bit when she arrives, to observe; if you see your son having a ball, it may reassure you that this is a positive arrangement for him, too, which makes any feelings of being taken advantage of less relevant. But no matter how well the children get along, the situation may wear thin if it happens too often, not to mention the added wear and tear on your house—or your nerves.

BETRAYALS AND BLUNDERS

I told my babysitter in confidence that I was concerned about my ten-year-old daughter's weight. We talked about ways to control the snacks and foods in the house—and I asked her not to bring up the issue in front of her. Next day I overheard her say to my daughter, "You can't have that, you're getting too fat."

Two strikes against her. First off, she showed a lack of tact and sensitivity in that she said something hurtful to your daughter— and for a caregiver that's poor form. Secondly, she either forgot or flagrantly ignored your gag order. Assuming the former, reiterate your desire that she not say anything to the child—it's possible you weren't as clear as you thought, and she felt she was actually being helpful. If, after talking to the sitter, you believe her motives were good, offer her some concrete ways to really help—like taking your daughter to the rollerblade rink. But if your child starts being overly conscious about her weight and starts making self-deprecating comments about herself at meal-time, say, or when looking in the mirror, there's a good chance you know the source—the sitter. An innocent blunder is one thing; a pattern of meanness is another, one that calls the whole relationship into question.

A few weeks ago I told my nanny, during a conversation about scheduling and salary, that it was possible my husband was going to be laid off. I never expected the information to leave our domain, but several days later I ran into a neighbor in the building, who said with concern, "I'm sorry to hear about your husband's job. . . ."

If you want something kept in confidence or within the inner circle of your home, you have to say so loud and clear; otherwise, there's no guarantee in this world that, given the opportunity, people—nannies or whomever—won't gossip. It's human nature, after all. If you feel you *were* direct, then you're best off bringing the subject up with the sitter—not in a confrontational way, but as a matter of clarification. You could say, "I'm guessing you told at least one person about my husband's job situation, since it's come back to me. I let you in on it because you may be directly affected, but it's not the sort of thing the world needs to know. So, in the future, let's keep family matters within the family." By emphasizing a sense of inclusion rather than pushing her away with admonishments, you're more apt to tap her sense of loyalty. If you're happy with her in most other regards, chalk the experience up to live and learn: You've learned that you should watch what you say or how you say it (emphasizing in no uncertain terms how secret a secret is); she's learned that blabber can boomerang.

Overheard: Running a Daycare Behind My Back

We hired a super-competent nanny to watch our seven-year-old son in the afternoons. She came in at twelve to walk the dog, do some laundry, meet our son's school bus, and entertain him until we got home. Bit by bit I noticed that she was getting less laundry done, and the house wasn't looking as pulled together. I knew one reason: She was having another boy in the building—a child of my son's age—come over in the afternoon to play, and that was fine. It started as a once-a-week thing, then my son told me his friend was coming over every day—and he said that sometimes when he wanted to go out and play the sitter said, no they had to wait for this friend. Then, one day in the elevator, I ran into another mother in the building who has three young girls, and she commented on how great our babysitter was. The mother seemed surprised that I had no idea her three girls were spending from noon to two o'clock in my apartment. It slowly dawned on me: My nanny was triple-dipping. I was paying her ten dollars an hour; so was the boy's mother, and so was the woman in the elevator. I felt so taken that I didn't even bother to give her the benefit of the doubt. I asked her to leave at the end of the week, and that was the last any of us in the building saw of her.

Chapter 11

The Small Stuff

Live or work in close proximity to someone, and it's almost impossible not to get annoyed by little quirks, of personality or physicality. Every parent, it seems, has a pet peeve, or a list of them, about something the sitter does or doesn't do. Complaining, you might say, is part of the territory; it goes along with kvetching about the husband, boss, neighbor, kids, or dog. Most of the time, the kinds of irritants that get under the skin are pretty innocuous, and unrelated to a person's capabilities as a caregiver—as in: She mumbles when you ask her a question, so you have to ask again; she hums off-key all day long; she's an inveterate snacker, leaving a trail of crumbs wherever she goes.

By voicing your annoyance, you risk hurting a nanny's feelings and, possibly, your relationship with her. On the other hand, if the "thing" is truly irksome and you *don't* bring it up, the little nothing may snowball and get so big that it blinds you to all the things you liked about your nanny in the first place. In some cases, your sitter may be unaware that she's doing something aggravating—like turning the radio up too loud—simply because you haven't said a word.

The behaviors that are most easily addressed and modified are those directly related to the kids and the job. Here you're on solid ground. Let's say the babysitter has a way of calling from the subway platform to tell you she's going to be late, when she already *is*. Or she hovers over you while you try to spend a few minutes with your child "alone" before leaving for work. Or say she loves to watch and report on sensationalist daytime talk shows. Or swears without thinking twice. These are the sort of offenses that don't usually warrant a firing, but do call for a friendly conversation.

Keep in mind, however, that there will be times when you should bite your tongue. After all, some things a person can't help. Forget, for example, about trying to change taste or style, let alone a person's sense of humor. It doesn't work. If a babysitter dresses, talks, walks, or sees the world in a certain way, try to live with it. You can be sure there are things about you that bother her.

LITTLE IRRITANTS

My sitter, who is from the West Indies, is always comparing her way of doing things with the American way, which comes off as critical and know-it-all. She'll say things like, "We don't get dressed in front of small children." Or "children should always wear shoes indoors."

When someone flouts your way of doing things, it's only natural to get a little defensive. For a lot of people, those kinds of challenging statements send out a signal to dig in one's heels and stand one's ground. But answering the nanny's bossiness with your own obstinance is counterproductive. After you've made a token "there are lots of ways to skin a cat" statement, try to detach yourself and not take her comments personally. Still, if you find that each and every time she remarks on the "right" way to do something you assume an adversarial position, that's not healthy for the relationship as a whole. You might need to reconsider whether you're right for each other.

It so happens that our sitter's favorite perfume is heavy, and the scent lingers long after she's left, in the house and on my newborn's skin. She wears it—a lot of it—all the time. I asked her once if she could tone it down, but she bristled and stubbornly continues to wear it anyway.

This is a two-layer irritation: First, she's wearing a strong perfume you hate; and second, she continues to wear it even though you asked her to go easy. Flagrant disregard for your wishes never feels good, but before you start looking for a scent-free, acquiescent sitter, ask again—clearly. You may have soft-pedaled your original request in an effort to be polite. If she continues to take a no-compromise stand—say she won't try a different scent—then that doesn't bode well for her give-and-take in other situations.

Nanny Point of View: Running Late

"My boss has an annoying habit of calling five minutes before she's supposed to be home to tell me she'll be just a few minutes late. The few minutes end up being more like fifteen or twenty. And because she's never late by more than half an hour, I don't feel comfortable asking for compensation. But it does screw me up. I have people waiting for me, too, and in the middle of rush hour I end up getting home later, sometimes much later than planned. I know she's not trying to be mean—she's absent-minded by nature, but I don't think she realizes how that affects me."

My sitter guzzles two or three giant liters of Coke a day, even though I made it clear that my six-year-old daughter isn't allowed to drink soda. I thought the sitter would understand that chugging Coke would not make her a great role model.

If your six-year-old isn't actually drinking the stuff, there's been no breaking of the rule. You can't police everything that goes on, including someone's choice of drink (imagine if your boss or your spouse suddenly put a moratorium on coffee or tea). If it's the aesthetic of the giant plastic containers that offends you or seems to make the habit more distasteful, think small and discreet: Ask the sitter to buy little individual bottles and/or to drink from a glass—not on the grounds that you disapprove of her vice, but as an example of good manners for the young and impressionable in the house.

Nanny Point of View: The Cupboard Is Bare

"My boss makes a big deal of saying, help yourself to anything in the refrigerator. But there's hardly a thing to eat. A carton of yogurt, some carrot sticks, skim milk, and some cheese and bread. She and her husband eat all their meals out or get takeout, and the baby has his jarred food. There are only so many days I can eat grilled cheese. I've started bringing my own lunch, but it's a pain to fix it when I'm rushing to work in the morning, not to mention the fact that all the nannies I know get to eat good food out of a well-stocked fridge."

It seems that whenever the phone rings, the call is for our sitter—her friends, her cousins, or her boyfriend—and she seems to have a lot to say to all of them. I don't want to be mean-spirited, but the calls are irritating.

Whether it's the constant ringing of the phone that grates (or having your phone calls interrupted by call-waiting beeps), or you're annoyed at being cast in the role of ad-hoc secretary or bugged that she's not more wired into the job and doing something kid-related, then do what bosses in the regular workplace do: Ask her to limit personal calls to two or three per day.

A MOODY STREAK

Our caregiver is wonderful in almost every way—except that she sometimes seems morose. She'll often come in to work head bent, shoulders slumped, like she's carrying the weight of the world. I understand everyone has off days, but I wish she were more consistently "up."

It should be part of her job to put her best face forward when she arrives in the morning. If a nanny seems down, then ask her if there's something about the work that's not working for her. A lot of parents don't *want* to ask—they don't want to get into it, and into the negatives of the relationship; likewise, they don't really want to know if there are "problems at home." They just want things to get magically better on their own. What's most important is how she is with the kids. Does she bring her moodiness to bear on her interactions with them? Does she eventually shift into cheerful mode, even if it takes an hour? Some nannies are simply not morning people—if this is the case, you'll have to accept it as part of the package.

WATCHING HER LANGUAGE

My husband and I make it a point to curb the curses around our four-year-old daughter, but she's suddenly taken to swear-

ing a blue streak and I'm afraid she's picked up the colorful new words from our sitter.

Unless *you* overhear the nanny dishing out the language, don't assume that she's the only source. Your daughter could be repeating four-letter words, not to mention colloquial phrases like "poopy head," that she's heard from kids on the playground or at preschool. In any case, you should broach the subject with your sitter, as in: "Molly has been using a lot of swear words lately— I don't know where she's getting them from, but if you hear the source, could you tell me?" Assuming the phase passes, you may never know whether the nanny began watching her mouth or the habit just died a natural death. And you probably won't care.

Overheard: The English Lesson

My sitter's grammar is not always perfect. She'll say "It don't matter" or "Where your socks?" After she'd worked with us six months or so, my two-and-a-half-year-old son began aping her. I'd find myself cringing every time he misspoke, but I wasn't at all comfortable correcting her grammar—it's too sensitive a subject. So what I'd do instead is correct my son's grammar, often in front of the nanny, hoping she'd pick up on my concern for proper usage herself. At first I felt a little ashamed that I wasn't being very direct. But I figured that it's pretty tough to change a grown-ups' way of talking, and my son seemed to have no problem relearning. In the final analysis, it didn't seem worth hurting her feelings over. I realized that between school and me, he'd be fine.

MEDIA POLICY

As soon as our newborn nods off, the sitter sits glued to the TV, watching the soaps. I'd rather she relaxed by reading a magazine or a book, or at least do something more productive.

It's probably not that you feel she's neglecting your child (who, after all, is blissfully asleep), but that you're annoyed at paying her to watch TV. If that's so, suggest she accomplish some mindless task while she watches, like ironing or folding clothes. If it's the subject matter that offends your sense of high culture, lay off—the show isn't damaging your little one, not at this stage anyway (of course, when the children are older, it's entirely appropriate to play media police). But if it's the noise of the tube that disturbs, the solution is simple. It's your house and your prerogative to lay down the law. No TV. Period.

Our nanny is an avid tabloid reader. Her bag is always bulging with a stash of the weekly papers, and she's quick to read the latest sensational headlines to our five-and eight-year olds, which doesn't strike me as appropriate.

A number of parents complain that their nannies have a taste for the lurid—and a need to share the most mawkish or shocking stories, whether from supermarket tabloids, TV talk shows, or the goriest news reports. You may not be comfortable playing censor with the nanny, but if you find that your kids are disquieted by what they're hearing—for example, they start obsessing about a kidnapping ten states away or are afraid to fly after learning every detail of a plane crash—it's well within bounds to ask the sitter to edit out the scary stuff. Or better yet, ask her to get all her "news" at home.

Overheard: Discordant Notes

Last year my sitter and I were locked in an epic power struggle over music. I'd set the kitchen radio to a news station while I was eating breakfast. As soon as she'd come in, I'd go out to do errands, and when I'd stop home later I'd find she'd changed the station to country, which drives me up the wall. I'd switch it back, then go off for the afternoon only to find when I came home in the early evening, she'd changed it again. One day I became so irritated, I snapped that she should just leave the radio alone. She said, no problem, but then she sulked for weeks. I felt badly that I was so abrupt, and told her what I really meant was that she could listen to whatever she wanted when I wasn't around, as long as she reset the station before I came home. But she kept "forgetting" to do that. The radio became our battleground. Before I even got home, I'd anticipate opening the front door and being assaulted by loud twangs. It was my seven-year-old daughter who came up with the solution: We bought the sitter a portable radio with headphones for her to use when we're not around. Now I don't care what she listens to—I never hear it.

Chapter 12

Safe and Sane

One of the biggest leaps we take as parents is in trusting that when we walk out the door, our kids are safe in the nanny's care. Will she remember to close the gate at the top of the stairs? Will she take the child's hand as they cross the street? Will she lose her temper and hit or shake a baby? When we read and hear about highly publicized cases of babysitters who hurt their charges, our anxiety levels and our antennae are raised. The more you think about what *could* happen, the scarier the proposition of even leaving the house becomes.

But don't let yourself go down that road too often. Once doubt and fear creep in, overprotectiveness is around the corner. You can't keep kids imprisoned; they're going to want to go to the park, the library, on play dates. And you don't want to circumscribe your own life by constantly hovering close to home. On some very elemental level, you need to have confidence in the caregiver—her sense of judgment and responsibility, and her overall character.

And you have to trust your nanny out there in the world. The very logistics of navigating a city can terrify some parents, who don't let their sitters and kids take subways or buses (walking distance can, after all, encompass a variety of venues). More often, however, parents allow for the necessity of public transportation, with the proviso that they keep to major routes.

In the suburbs or in rural areas, driving is the main issue—and for most parents, a major requirement. A nanny with a license is an invaluable asset: She can pick the kids up from school or soccer practice or do the weekly grocery shopping. But again, some parents would rather not bring the third-party risk into the picture, and insist on doing all the driving themselves.

Even when nanny and kids are presumably safe at home, there are worries that can rattle parents—anything from falling off a bunk bed to choking on a grape. You can offset a lot of angst by taking the sitter on a walk through the house, in which you go over every potential pitfall—and every persnickety concern. Be up-front about your particular fears, whether it's about drowning in the tub or falling out a window. If knowing that the sitter can do the Heimlich maneuver would make you feel more comfortable, then enroll your nanny in an emergency first aid course (and pay for it, plus her time). A lot of parents take the class along with the caregiver, which helps to reinforce the training and spreads the sense of responsibility among all the adults; if only one of you knows CPR, you're counting on the trained person being there in an emergency. Even a nanny who comes with a CPR certificate may need a refresher class, especially since techniques—which differ for babies, toddlers, and children—are sometimes revised.

Accidents aside, the fear of abuse—physical, psychological, or sexual—lurks in many parents' minds, even without evidence or just cause. Most parents can distinguish a scratch or cut suffered in a fall at the playground from a squeezed-arm bruise (if not, a doctor certainly can), but there is a whole spectrum of ambiguous symptoms of mistreatment, including signs of verbal abuse. Re-

peated complaints from a child about a sitter's behavior—
"Jeanie's so mean to me"—can put a parent on guard, and rightly
so. Some scenarios are so obviously egregious, they call for dismissal without a second thought or a second chance: witnessed
punching, slapping, kicking, licking, or fondling, or other risky
though nonabusive acts, such as letting a six-year-old drive the
car in the driveway or leaving a nine-year-old alone at a local
shopping center for an hour.

Not surprisingly, in this age of high nanny anxiety, some parents resort to spying to get their proof or reassurance—and there
are plenty of companies ready to provide hidden video cameras.
Occasionally, parents are simply curious to see how a nanny and
child interact unsupervised (like in an observation room at a
preschool, and find comfort in witnessing a loving and playful
relationship. But if you're at the point where you're seriously considering a covert operation, you probably have enough doubt
about your nanny's competence that you already know what you
need to do.

THE ANXIOUS PARENT

**Even though our nanny's been with us for a year, and I think
she's terribly competent, I still haven't been able to relax fully
when I'm away from my daughter. I keep envisioning everything that could go wrong, from being hit by a cab to being
abducted while the nanny looks the other way for a second.**

You're one of millions. Leaving a child in the care of someone
other than a close relative can make a parent feel powerless and
vulnerable. Risk, unfortunately, is inherent in moving through
the world. But while some events are clearly not in your control,
like lightning striking or a brick falling off a building, you can
take precautions that will put your mind a bit more at ease, such

as making sure the nanny knows the pediatrician's number and the neighbors' numbers, where the fire extinguisher is kept and the emergency money is stashed. Some parents provide the nanny with a signed note that authorizes her, in the case of a life-threatening accident, to make emergency decisions if they can't be reached (a safety measure to bypass the red tape of hospitals that won't make a move without signed consent). Worrywarts may never be entirely at peace with the notion of childcare—they have to learn to live with the anxiety.

Our sitter has made a few mistakes lately—forgetting to pack a lunch for our daughter and being late two days in a row to pick up our son at school. It makes me worry whether she's starting to "lose it."

These aren't capital offenses and they may not even be much to worry about. Everyone spaces out once in a while—forgets where they put their keys or where they parked the car—because they're tired or temporarily preoccupied. But lapses in memory during childcare duty are more worrisome. If the sitter's behavior is suddenly, markedly, spacey you may need to ask that classic question: "Is everything okay at home?" There may be something that needs her attention (marital stress, health problems)—and if so, better to solve it sooner rather than later. Clearly, if the incidents are upsetting to the children or offend your own sense of responsibility, she needs to make a real effort to reform. The old note-taped-to-the-refrigerator trick may help her remember the lunch or remind her to leave extra time to get where she's going, so as not to disappoint anyone.

Overheard: The Nanny and Kids Are AWOL

The sitter took our toddler and baby uptown to the zoo in the morning. I had asked her to be back with the kids in the afternoon, but by the time it was getting dark there was still no sign of them. I agonized for an hour about whether to call the police. And then at six-thirty, they burst through the door, happy and full of tales from their day's adventure. The nanny said they were having a great time and she didn't call home because she had just enough change for the bus and not a cent extra for the phone. Mixed with my relief that they were fine was a good dose of resentment. Excuses aside, I felt our sitter made some pretty lousy decisions. If she didn't have the money to reach me, she should have gotten home at the agreed time. And if she wanted to stay out, she could have shown more resourcefulness by calling collect. No matter how much she apologized, she had shaken my confidence in her. I told her quite honestly, "I don't know if I can get over this—just go home." The next morning I had cooled down and was willing to give her a second chance, with the clear understanding that if I had to go through that kind of anxiety again, I'd regretfully let her go.

JUDGING HER JUDGMENT

My sitter has apparently taken it upon herself to make sure my fifteen-month-old daughter will not be afraid of heights. She's been teaching her how to jump off the changing table, which my daughter did one day when I was barely looking.

Applaud the motivation—your nanny's obviously taking an active role in more than feeding and changing your daughter. But then step back and look at her actions. Table jumping may be in the nanny's repertoire of tricks, something she says she's successfully taught her other charges without incident or injury, but the risk outweighs the potential benefits—not to mention that this kind of "lesson" should have been cleared with you in advance. The average fifteen-month-old is unable to distinguish three feet from ten feet, and you certainly don't want her suddenly cata-pulting off every piece of furniture in the house. You don't have to undercut her instructor enthusiasm, but you do want to un-derscore her protective role (including protecting her job) by say-ing something like, "When I'm at work, I don't want to be thinking about an accident waiting to happen. So no table jump-ing, please, unless I'm there to catch her."

The other day when I left for work, my son was coming down with the flu and running a temperature of 101 degrees. I told our caregiver to call me if his fever went up, and we'd decide whether to go to the doctor. When I got home I found out they'd made a trip to the doctor's after all, even though the baby was clearly much better.

This is a case where the nanny showed more good judgment than bad. Even if she erred on the side of caution, that's better than the reverse. In fact, a more common complaint among parents is about the nanny who is too passive rather than too take-charge. If she's an experienced mother and/or sitter, you have to trust that she has some pretty well-honed instincts—and you're only out the cost of the doctor's visit. If she's a novice and you sense she acted out of panic, not competence, make sure the house rules are clear: The next time there's a health issue, you'll be the one to decide when it's better safe than sorry.

Our kids are pretty grown up and independent for seven- and nine-year-olds—but I was surprised the other day when I got home from work early to find them in the house on their own.

The nanny, who showed up in the car twenty minutes later, mumbled something about running out to pick up milk.

You probably assumed it was an understood rule that children are never left alone; your sitter may have thought school-age kids are mature enough to handle a short time solo. And, in fact, the sitter may come from a family or culture in which kids were left to care for each other at young ages. These are the kinds of issues that need to be hammered out early—sometimes it takes a nerve-wracking incident to bring the discussion up. But if this is something you talked expressly about and she breached a household law, then it will be hard to trust her word again.

Overheard: The Black-Paint Fiasco

The other day, my three-year-old son had a friend over for a play date. I was working in my home office and the nanny was supervising the boys, who were outside running around. At some point they went into the shed where we store a lot of outdoor toys. On a shelf in the back they found an old can of black oil paint and managed to pry the top off and cover themselves in the sticky stuff. Their hands and arms were completely black and they'd splattered paint on their faces and in their hair. The nanny knocked on my office door and calmly told me I'd better come outside. When I saw the boys, I panicked. I had no idea how to get them clean, although I knew enough not to use turpentine. Meanwhile, the nanny got a bucket and soap, and when it was clear the paint wasn't budging, she suggested we call the 800 number on the paint can. The antidote turned out to be vegetable oil; each of us grabbed a bottle and went to work for the next hour. She then bathed both boys and dressed them in clean T-shirts and jeans. When the friend's mom came to pick up her son, she wouldn't have known anything had happened, except for the bag of ruined clothes.

Our sitter's remarkable calm was contagious—once the boys knew she wasn't flustered, they relaxed, and so did I. But that's not to say she brushed the incident off casually. Later that night, she called to say she was obviously still thinking about the day; she called to say she hoped she'd gotten all the paint out of my son's hair, but just in case, to put something down on his pillow.

WHO'S BEHIND THE WHEEL?

Our new sitter has her driver's license—that was one of our requirements—but how can I judge how good a driver she really is without obviously "testing" her?

There's nothing wrong with checking her driving skills. And there's no need to apologize for it, either. Ask her to take you for a little spin around town. Is she heavy on the accelerator or the brake? Does she drift through stop signs? Does she park a mile from the curb? Even if she's not the smoothest driver on the planet, do you feel safe?—that's the bottom line. If it's her own car she'll be using to chauffeur the kids, take the test drive in her vehicle to check out its running condition and the level of basic cleanliness— if it's a real rust-bucket rattler (or pig sty) you may prefer she use your car. For her edification and your comfort level, also take her through a dry run of places she's likely to be driving to and from— school, grocery store—as well as down any tricky one-way streets and through traffic circles, speed traps, or notorious curves.

I want to have the nanny drive the kids in our car—but what would happen if she were in an accident? Would we be liable?

In most states, anyone who drives your car—whether it's a family member, nanny, or the teenager down the street—is covered by your insurance policy, but it's certainly worth checking with your insurance agent. (If household employees are excluded, you'll want to add the nanny's name as an additional insured at what's probably a negligible cost.) When she's driving *her* car on *your* time, however, it's a different and more complicated story. Say she plows down a stop sign or wrecks another car on her way to pick up the kids at school. The law in most states holds an employer liable for any accident caused by an employee while on the job—which means you could be held responsible for damages that exceed the nanny's insurance coverage. The moral: Make sure the nanny's personal auto insurance has the same type of coverage as does the family's—that is, plenty. Then there's the psychological weight of self-blame in the event of an accident, especially one involving a child—the feeling of being haunted by the things you could have controlled (if you only had checked the tires, the brakes). You can't buy a policy on that. The only way to cover every possible eventuality is to do all the driving yourself.

Although all my friends have caregivers, I can't remember seeing one driving the carpool. Is it kosher to ask my sitter to drive for me when I'm too busy?

You're lucky to have back-up, but you should definitely let the other mothers know. Some parents feel strongly, for whatever reason, that a nanny's place is not behind the wheel, and may opt out of the carpool that day (though if you think about it, a nanny isn't really a bigger risk than another parent whose driving skills may be equally unknown). In any case, if the sitter does participate, set clear ground rules—for example, no kids in the front seats, or way in the back if you've got a van or station wagon; kids under four need to be in car seats; no traveling on the highway or other high-speed roads; no blasting the radio (it can be distracting, especially in concert with screaming kids); no eating or drinking (to avoid spills, gagging, or choking); and if her car is unreliable in any way, she must use the family auto. One last detail: It's only fair to ask the nanny if *she* is comfortable being responsible for a carload of kids.

DRIVING MADLY AND BADLY

I sent my nanny on a simple driving mission: to take my daughters to play with kids five blocks away. After half an hour the mother called and said, "Are your girls coming?" Thirty minutes later the nanny arrived home with the kids in tears, the play date abandoned.

Some people have a natural sense of direction; plenty of people don't. If you're one of the latter, it's easy to lose your way in just a few unfamiliar miles. In any case, to avoid a replay of mishaps, write the directions down, including not just street names but also visual landmarks (the big white house with the green trim, the stone church on the corner). It's always a good idea to keep a town map in the car and a roll of quarters for emergency calls. Obviously, if you have a phone in the car, you're covered—as long as she feels free to use it and knows the code.

My nanny sheepishly told me she got a speeding ticket while driving our car. She was on her way to pick up the kids at softball practice, and was afraid she'd be late. She apologized profusely, but now I'm uneasy about having her chauffeur everybody around.

It's the rare adult who hasn't ever been busted for speeding. The real issue here is, how fast was she going? Driving double the speed limit—fifty miles per hour in a twenty-five miles per hour area, say—doesn't bode well for her sense of judgment. And if she gets too many tickets, she could have her license revoked, which is in no one's interest. But if she was going within ten or so miles of the speed limit and you feel she is by and large a cautious driver, the best course is to have her pay up and let it go. Consider, however, whether the speeding is a symptom of a different problem—namely, her inability to correctly gauge how long it will take her to get from point A to point B. You may have to stay on top of her schedule for a while, giving a specific time to leave ("You'll need to head out by four to get to the softball field on time").

URBAN TRANSIT

We live in a city where taxis and subways are the usual mode of transport. I'm a little nervous about having the nanny handle the kids on public transportation.

When it comes to subways, the most treacherous part of the ride is dealing with the crowd. For platform safety, impress upon your nanny that she and the child must stand against a wall, as far away as possible from the track. With a baby or toddler, the stroller is a must—it keeps the child from running off or getting lost. And although it's a bit awkward to lug the stroller up and down the subway stairs, a city nanny is usually adept at maneuvering—or at recruiting help. As for taxis, some parents insist the nanny haul a car seat into cabs, but that's a hassle, and it's simply not practical if she's got a stroller to handle, too. With an infant, have the sitter wear the baby in a papoose-type carrier and buckle up over the carrier. Toddlers under four should sit in the nanny's lap in the center back seat, considered the safest seat in the car, and buckle the seat belt over their two laps. And have the sitter lock both doors—curious toddlers will inevitably want to try out all the buttons and handles. Kids over four can sit on their own, belted in. City buses present a peculiar situation in that there are no safety belts; not much a nanny can do except keep an arm hold on the kid, since a sudden lurch can send a child flying into the aisle.

The Unspeakables

I've let our nanny know that there's no yelling or spanking in our house. But when I got home last night, she told me our daughter had bitten her, leaving a dark bruise. Then she said, half jokingly, that all my daughter needs is a little spanking.

If she was half joking, she was also half serious. Assuming you've had the discussion previously, you have every right to be concerned. Even though she's followed the letter of the law you laid down, she hasn't embraced the spirit. She may have different ideas about discipline—and that's okay when it's her own kid she's dealing with; but the fact that she brought the subject up with you means she's in some way challenging your approach. And while no employer wants to feel she has to convince an employee to adopt her philosophies, you want to feel secure that the employee is putting your wishes first—in this or any arena.

The woman who babysits part time for us is wonderful with our kids. But the other day my youngest, who is three, asked me to lick her toes like the sitter does. I was taken aback, to say the least.

It's one thing to kiss a baby's feet, but there's definitely something more sexual about sucking toes. If this is the only odd thing that's ever come up, be direct: Ask the sitter if she knows what the new licking toes thing is all about—maybe it's a kissing-counting game or something equally benign. But if this is one in a series of weird or unexplained stories, your parental instincts may be telling you something and guiding you to make a change of caregiver.

My two-year-old son has very fair skin—every little bruise shows up. Still, it seems like he's had more than his usual share of accidents lately. I know bumps and scrapes are the stock-in-trade of childhood, but how can I tell if any are suspicious?

As a doctor will tell you, bruises on the lower leg and lower arm—even when there are several—are easily attributed to normal routine falls. More troubling are bruises in unlikely places, such as the back, upper arm, neck. Generally speaking, if there's physical abuse you'll see other signs as well. Some of the classic tip-offs, say experts, include extreme mood swings, withdrawal, a sudden fear of people, and out-of-the-blue bed-wetting. The first person to talk to is the nanny—not in an accusatory way since, after all, you don't know what's happened—but simply as parent to caregiver, for example, "Where do you think this big bruise on his shoulder came from?" A plausible explanation—a camera fell off the counter and hit him—can set your mind at ease. But don't lose the opportunity to talk about the incident. Tell the nanny you'd like to be informed of when and how these minor accidents occur. A string of them raises another, no less troubling question: Is this sitter properly supervising your child?

Overheard: The Nanny Accused

We recently moved to the suburbs from the city and our much-loved nanny moved with us. I totally trusted her in all ways—which is why I initially became unglued when the director of our daughter's new preschool called me at the office to report an incident she observed with our nanny. The director said our sitter yanked our daughter by the arms, causing her pain; she was concerned enough that she thought about notifying the authorities. I immediately called home and heard a different story from the nanny.

As she told it, they got to school early, and my daughter was getting antsy and rambunctious waiting for the school day to start. She began climbing up and jumping off a tall table onto a concrete floor. After telling her it wasn't a safe thing to do, our nanny swung her down from the table and set her on her feet. That was it. The nanny was angry that she'd been accused of mistreating our daughter—and she was enraged that the school contemplated calling the police. The next morning she met with the director, laid out the situation from her viewpoint—and cleared her name. The incident only served to increase my respect for—and commitment to—our nanny.

A Quick Study: Spying on Nanny

Since the 1997 trial of Boston au pair Louise Woodward, who was convicted of manslaughter in the death of an infant, ads for nanny video-surveillance services have popped up all over the Web and in the backs of parenting magazines. Putting ethics aside for a moment, there is something irresistible about the prospect of observing, covertly, the interaction between child and care-giver—that fly-on-the-wall temptation to see what goes on when your son doesn't want to take a nap or refuses to eat lunch or begs to watch more TV. Dealers in the video-surveillance market play on parents' natural curiosity—and play up the fear aspect, pointing out how unregulated the childcare industry is in this country, and how reports of abusive caretakers have turned up on various TV talk and news shows.

If you're tempted to tune into the caregiver's day there are any number of ways to spy: with a camera hidden in a coffee pot, an alarm radio, a cell phone, or a smoke detector. Average price for the setup: $200 and up for a three-day rental. Once the surveillance is completed, the agency takes back the hidden camera and leaves you with hours of tapes. As for invasion of privacy, the visual portion of videotapes is legal (meaning you don't need to inform a nanny). The audio, however, is trickier—some states forbid eavesdropping without notifying the subject beforehand. A call to your state legislature will clarify the law.

So what are parents likely to witness? Not, thankfully, out-and-out abuse. The most common "crime," say people who operate surveillance services, is benign neglect—for example, massive amounts of TV watching or phone talking. Short of firing the nanny or coming right out and telling her what you've seen, and risking her rage and immediate walkout, you can attempt to modify the lax behavior through the power of suggestion. You might mention, for example, that you're on a new mission to eliminate all daytime TV watching by all family members. This approach, of course, requires a follow-up spying session.

Fifty to seventy percent of the nannies who have been spied upon end up being fired. The figures may be this high, of course, because the group of parents who arrange for surveillance in the first place are usually those who are already on the road to letting the nanny go.

Part V

Close Quarters

Chapter 13

Is the Nanny Coming to Thanksgiving?

Just because you're paying someone a salary doesn't guarantee a businesslike relationship. In fact, it's nearly impossible to maintain total distance in a domestic setting. The tricky part, for many people, is where to draw the line. Some like to feel that a nanny is a part of the family, so much so that they invite her to share holiday meals, go to the kids' recitals, birthdays, and graduations, and let her in on all their trials and tribulations.

This familial attitude has its upsides. For one thing, treating an employee as a family member can assuage any guilt you may have about the notion of paying someone to look after your children. For those who are uncomfortable with the notion of domestic help the friendly family approach shoves the issue under the rug. Then there's the parents' personality to take into account: People who are naturally informal and outgoing tend to encourage casual relationships, whether it's with a nanny, a secretary, or a mail carrier; reticent, private, or otherwise more reserved people are prone to play their cards close to the chest. Some people simply love to be part of a group dynamic; the feeling of being one big, happy family is reinforcing to everyone involved. Give a sitter—especially a live-in—several years with in one household, and often the ties become so strong that it's easy to forget when and where the relationship began; it simply is and always was.

But while some families grow quite fond of their caregivers, and vice versa, no one should feel remiss if that fuzzy feeling doesn't happen. You can be perfectly satisfied with the love and care a sitter gives a child without needing to get it or give it yourself. Besides, closeness, as nice as it is, often comes with its own set of drawbacks. The most common complaint is a lack of boundaries—once they're blurred, it's hard to redraw them. Many parents smudge the lines between caregiver and "relative" or "friend" without even realizing it. They find themselves babbling to their nannies, telling them all about their day at work, their problems with their in-laws. But a nanny is not a hairstylist or therapist who you don't see again until the next appointment. Not only are you potentially burdening her with stuff she doesn't want to know, you're revealing a lot about yourself, which you may regret at some later date—what if, for example, the nanny leaves and goes to work for a friend of a friend or a colleague? Once you divulge, you also open the door for the nanny to use you as a sounding board—sharing intimate details about her husband, kids, personal finances. If you'd rather not know, hold back—before you get too close for comfort.

THE AWKWARD INVITATION

I'm toying with the idea of inviting my nanny to Thanksgiving dinner. She doesn't have relatives nearby, and I don't like to think of her sitting alone. On the other hand, it seems a little odd to include her in such a family-oriented holiday.

Don't presume it will be uncomfortable for her (even if for you, it's another story). Of all holidays, Thanksgiving traditionally extends itself to friends, friends of friends, near strangers, whoever happens to be in town. Your nanny, whose own relatives are distant, may well be used to sitting at others' tables. Much of the dynamic depends on the nature of the gathering—big, casual, boisterous, family-style groups tend to absorb extras better than small, family-members-only sit-down affairs. In any case, if you decide for whatever reason *not* to ask, don't dwell on it—it's only one day of the year.

My son is celebrating his first birthday with a few friends and family members. The party is on a Saturday, and I don't know whether to invite the sitter or not—and whether to pay or not.

It's a nice gesture to invite the nanny, as long as you don't mind throwing her in the middle of friends and family, whom she may not know well or at all. If you decide to include her, the next question is, are you asking her as a guest (in which case you wouldn't pay her); or are you asking her to come and help out (in which case you would pay a regular hourly wage). Either way, you're obliged to cover her transportation or give her a lift—after all, she's coming over in the middle of the day for what's essentially a piece of cake. Nannies themselves are split about whether they like being asked to intimate events. Those who have a close bond with the child may feel hurt at being left out; others, who like to keep a certain distance, may feel compelled to say yes, even if they'd rather not interrupt their day off. So ask, and try to read between the lines. The last thing you want is a disgruntled sitter at a birthday party.

Nanny Point of View: RSVP-ing

"I enjoy being included in family events, but sometimes the invitation sounds hollow—like they think they have to ask me—and then I'm not sure if they really want me to say yes. A few times I've gone, only to sit by myself while it seemed like everyone looked at me a little warily, as if to say, 'What is she doing here.'"

FAMILY AFFAIRS

My eight-year-old daughter is performing in a ballet recital and really wants her sitter to come and watch her. I don't love the idea—partly because of the money (forty-five dollars a ticket) and partly because I want to be able to focus on our daughter, not on whether the babysitter is having a good time. How can I please everybody?

The price of a ticket aside, many parents have trepidations about attending this kind of family event with an employee. There are a couple of tactful ways to get around the tricky situation without saying no to either your child or the sitter. One is to ask the nanny to a dress rehearsal; that way your daughter still gets to show off, and you get to go to opening night en famille. Another is simply to get her a ticket in a different row of the theater so you don't have to make small talk between acts. Some parents wonder whether they need to pay for the sitter's time if the performance takes place in the evening or on a weekend. The answer is, not usually. The more common practice is to buy her the ticket and leave it at that—it sends a strange message to all involved when you pay somebody to be part of an audience.

We want to take a week's vacation in Mexico, and we're considering bringing our caregiver. While it would be a great help

to have the extra eyes at the beach, I'm not sure I want to share meals and that kind of family time, or even to have her see me in my bathing suit.

This is a classic trade-off: Let her in, let her help, and you expose yourself—in more ways than one. Granted, having your regular nanny right there guarantees you won't be worrying about whether your kids are in good hands, which makes for a good vacation. But some parents feel that their family "alone time" is too precious to share. By adding another person to the mix, you certainly change the dynamic of the group. A less-intrusive setup can be had by arranging locally for a few hours a day of babysitting (through the hotel, most likely)—the anonymity may be easier to live with.

Overheard: An Extra Guest at the Seder Table

We always have Passover dinner at our house. This past holiday, it was a small group: my husband, my son, and my in-laws—with whom I don't have a very easy-going relationship (they tend to grill me on every subject from childcare to my career). It occurred to me to invite our nanny; I feel rather close to her and she's expressed interest in participating in a Seder. While I was sure that she would want to go, my motivation was partly selfish: I figured that having her there as my ally would tip the balance of the table, allowing me to deflect a lot of my in laws' questions and criticisms. As I predicted, she accepted the invitation, and her presence took me out of the hot seat; she got all the questions instead. The next day, we gossiped about how narrow-minded and pompous my in-laws are. That was fine, but the nanny didn't leave it at that. Over the next few months, she'd make snide comments whenever their names came up, and I realized that a line had been crossed. It was okay for me to complain about my own in-laws, but once she started doing *it, I felt oddly protective of them. I stopped responding to her jibes and bit my tongue whenever I felt like saying something nasty. Eventually the subject died out.*

BLURRED BOUNDARIES

I'm very happy with our nanny, except for her gossipy chatter. She tells me everything about her dating life, which makes me feel more like her girlfriend than her boss. While I sometimes get a little vicarious charge out of hearing the stories, I feel I'm destroying my credibility by taking part in the conversation.

Follow your instincts. If you want to maintain authority in day-to-day matters, you're best off keeping some distance. One danger with being a listener is the temptation to start talking: She mentions a fight with her boyfriend, you find yourself confiding in her about the one you had last night with your husband. Regardless of whether you divulge or not, there are some things you just don't want to hear from an employee—graphic sexual escapades, perhaps, or the story of her nose job. Once those intimate stories are out there, they hover between you—it's often hard to look at her the same way.

Nanny Point of View: More Than I Want to See

"One of my employers has taken a leave of absence from his job and he's been hanging around the house. I've worked for the family for two years, and I feel close to them. But this is going too far. He spends all morning lounging in his underwear. I find it inappropriate and rude—just because I'm around all the time, doesn't make me a member of the family, and it doesn't make me invisible."

My husband has been traveling a lot lately, and I find myself using the nanny as a sounding board—seeking her advice on what clothes go with what, giving her updates about my day at work, asking her whether I need a haircut. Sometimes I think about what I've said, and I'm sorry I said so much.

Some people are prone to live their lives out loud. Idle conversation is usually harmless; you just want to be sure you don't change unalterably the dynamic of a relationship that has been working well. Once you open new intimate territory, it's often difficult to step back—and take back the friendliness. But don't overthink the matter. Many employees are used to listening to their bosses babble on—it goes in one ear and out the other.

We rent a summer house near the ocean and spend most of our weekend time hanging out at the beach. I'm tempted to ask our new live-in to come along—to keep an eye on the kids while my husband and I swim, and also to enjoy herself. But I'm afraid it's not clear, to us or anyone, what her role would be—family member or employee.

Even though the ocean is vast, the outing may be rather close. Beaches (and other R & R locales) imply leisure time, so it's often hard to carry over normal boss-employee roles from home onto the sand. Part of the difficulty is that one or both parents are there—not working and off somewhere, leaving her in charge. And that means there are two or three caregivers sitting together: Are you and the nanny comfortable reading books side by side or making conversation? And which of you is going to get up and build the sandcastle or walk the toddler to the water's edge? Also tricky is whether you're asking her to join you at the beach on her day off. If so, make it clear she doesn't have to work but she'll most likely help you carry all the gear. If you ask and sense hesitation, don't push. A nanny who's uncomfortable at the beach (she doesn't swim, won't wear a bathing suit) is going to be out of her element—and that can lead to awkwardness all around.

COMING IN TOO CLOSE

My sitter has mentioned a few times that her husband is out of work. Even though she's pretty cheerful, I know they're going through a rough patch money- and marriage-wise. The problem is, I can't bring myself to ask how things are and I feel a little bad about not showing more interest.

No one really wants to be burdened with someone else's tales of woe. And besides, you may be using good judgment. It's presumptuous to assume that she needs your ear or advice. If, however, she brings the subject up, leaving the door open for discussion, let her unload a little. After all, most working people have colleagues at work to gripe to; unless a nanny gets together with a regular bunch of caregivers at the park, she's not going to have a chance for that water-cooler conversation. Sometimes you're the only one around to listen.

Nanny Point of View: Joining the Club

"My employer and I often end up reading the same books and comparing notes. The other day she surprised me by inviting me to join her book group. I was flattered, but not really that interested. I mean, all these women are fifteen years older than me, have kids, and make a lot more money. What would I have in common with them? Besides, I see her five days a week—why would I want to spend my evenings with her? I felt like she was pulling me in too much, closer than I wanted to be."

Our sitter has only worked for us for two months and already she's asking about my career, where my husband went to college, what my sister is naming her baby, and even about my own childbirth experiences. It's all happening too fast. I feel like she hasn't quite earned the right to know so much so soon.

The most natural kind of closeness is gradual and progressive. An aggressive pursuit of intimacy can be off-putting to a lot parents. In most cases, however, the sitter is simply eager to be accepted quickly. She's jumping into her member-of-the-family role with both feet, on the premise that the more she knows, the closer you'll feel to her—and she's unwittingly pushing the limits of acceptability in the process. As nannies settle in and become more secure, these cases of overenthusiasm are typically self-resolving. If you sense, however, that she's intrusive by nature, simply clam up ("I think that's too personal"). And if you suspect a more subversive motive lurks behind a false intimacy, then you'd best trust your gut that something is off. Call it a mother's instinct.

Our nanny is very maternal, which is great for our kids—but she turns it on me, too. She'll pick hairs off my sweater, advise me on my diet and clothes, and give me a big hug now and then.

You probably don't want the nanny to nanny you because it makes you another one of her charges and undercuts your parental authority. Or you feel that some of her actions, like straightening your collar, carry an implicit judgment. And for nontouchy-feely types, this kind of futzing is an invasion of privacy of the most basic kind. Still, there's not much you can do to change someone's basic nature—even if you could bring yourself to ask her to stop hugging you, she'd find other ways to express affection. In this kind of situation, when something or someone is good for the kids, it's worth finding a way to grin and bear it.

Overheard: When Knowing Less Is Better

When I hired my live-in sitter, I was vaguely aware of the fact she had a daughter about the same age as mine. Her daughter, she told me, lived with her aunt in Grenada, but that's about all she said. Occasionally, she'd mention her, and I'd realize with a start that not only did she have a daughter, but that I'd blanked out on the child's name. Eventually, after our nanny had been with us for two years, her daughter came to live in the States with cousins about twenty miles away. Sometimes our sitter brought her daughter, who was now nine, over to our house. Our daughter had fun hanging out with her—it was me who had the problem. Each time I saw the girl, I'd feel badly that her mother was leaving her with a relative while she lived with us during the week. I'd see the nanny making my kids dinner, tucking them into bed, and I'd think she could be home doing the same things with her own child. I realized that knowing this whole part of her personal life made it harder for me to keep my distance as a boss, because I started seeing her not as an employee, but as another mother. It was easier for me when I didn't know so much—so whenever the daughter came up in conversation, I found a way to not listen so closely.

Chapter 14

Living with a Live-in

On paper, the situation couldn't be better: Someone to take care of the kids day and night—someone who's always there in the morning, so you don't have to worry about whether you'll be late for an appointment because the sitter has overslept or is stuck on a subway; who's always there in the evening, so you don't have to rush to get home, bolting out of a meeting at 5:30, mumbling something about getting back to relieve the babysitter. It means you can have a life after work, without ever having to scramble to find a babysitter on short notice. And since you're providing room and board, you don't pay any more for all this valuable back-up—usually a little less, actually—than for a live-out sitter.

So what are the downsides? Potentially, plenty. First of all, you'd better really like the nanny since you'll be living under the same roof (which brings its own stresses and strains). And you'd better be willing to carve up some space for this additional member of the family. In the ideal scenario, you'd have a separate wing for a caregiver. But most families with live-ins make do with sur-prisingly limited accommodations—a spare room and, sometimes but not always, a separate bath. You have to think about the logistics of mealtime, too. Do you want to share the dinner hour? Or is she going to eat separately? And in the emotional scheme of things, realize that you're going to be held captive to her moods, not to mention any social and family sagas she brings to the table.

One of the fallacies about live-in help is that you've got round-the-clock coverage. Not quite. A live-in, though physically present for a five- or seven-day week, can't possibly be on call twenty-four hours, though some parents push the limits to the breaking point. The max should be fourteen hours per day (most parents cite twelve as standard) plus two full days off a week. Some parents like to establish a clear-cut time when the nanny's day begins and ends, from eight in the morning to eight at night, say, and what she's responsible for during the evening hours— making the kids dinner? Putting them to bed? Fixing school lunches for the next day? Other parents prefer a loose arrangement in which there's no set schedule and lots of room for give and take on both sides in terms of time and duties—a much more casual and communal approach to caregiving. And there are a zillion variations between these extremes. The one truism about live-ins is that you can't really generalize what works best because the dynamic is so dependent on the parents' lifestyle, the nanny's temperament, and the personality mix.

For all the pros and cons, the decision to hire a live-in seems to come down to how much you value privacy versus how much you need or depend on (or become accustomed to) a third hand. Parents seem to fall into two camps: Those who say, after several live-ins, that they want their house, their time, their family to themselves again; and those who, having once experienced the luxury of the live-in, can't imagine going back to a time when they had to think twice about sleeping in now and then or going to a movie on a whim.

Make Room for Nanny

We have one extra bedroom that we've fixed up for the live-in, who's starting next week. What else, besides meals, are we expected to cover?

There are two answers: One, what you *should* provide as the bare minimum (the room, three meals a day); and two, what's *in your own interest* to provide. Many parents give the sitter her own TV (so she doesn't have to watch with all of you all the time), and some even plug a small refrigerator into her room (so the family fridge isn't overrun with the sitter's sodas or nibbles, and she can keep some measure of independence, without having to trot back and forth to the kitchen for a snack). Setting a nanny up with her own phone, phone number, and answering machine also makes life easier for everyone. Employers usually pay for the equipment and basic service, and the nanny pays for her long-distance phone calls. Another perk (call it a necessity if you live in the 'burbs or the countryside) is the "nanny car"—a vehicle the sitter can use to shuttle the kids around or take herself out and about. Typically, the parents pay for all car expenses, including insurance and gas—although if the nanny takes off on weekend excursions, it's fair to ask her to refill the tank.

We're considering hiring a live-in sitter, and the word is that the salary tends to be less than for live-outs. But since we'll be providing room and board, won't it end up costing about the same in the end? Or more?

Not usually. Figure the room is there regardless. Yes, there's a certain amount that's added to the family load in terms of electricity, laundry, general wear and tear on the house—but that's hard to quantify and it's usually not worth trying. A nanny's portion of food can certainly add to the grocery bill, but the amount really depends on your culinary taste and hers, not to mention your mealtime arrangements: If you tend to spend a lot on serious food and she joins the table every evening, the added mouth can hike your costs by as much as fifty dollars a week. But if she eats with the kids and eats simple kid food, then we're talking peanuts. Keep in mind, too, that most live-out nannies eat breakfast and lunch on the job anyway, so it's really dinner that tips the scale. All told, in the end you're still laying out less for a live-in, plus you tend to get a little more out of the deal since live-ins' days tend to be longer and the hours more lenient.

Overheard: Loft Living with a Live-in

I initially resisted the idea of a live-in sitter for our son because we have an open loft with only two bedrooms and one bath. But I work long, somewhat unpredictable hours and have to travel quite a bit, and I hadn't interviewed a live-out sitter who could accommodate my crazy schedule. The woman we ended up hiring was interested in living in, and my husband and I liked her so much, we decided to give it a go. It's been two years, and we're all still talking— better yet, we're all pretty happy. The lack of privacy I so feared hasn't really been that much of a problem. Sure, there are times I wish we had more than one bathroom, but in the spirit of give-and-take, we've worked it out. I take my shower in the morning, my husband usually showers at the gym after his lunchtime workout, our son takes a bath before dinner, and our nanny takes hers before she turns in for the night. Up until now, she's shared the bedroom with my son—she had the bed, he had the crib—but now that he's ready to move into a real bed himself, we're looking at creating an extra room for her in the loft. In

terms of evening hours—the time I thought I'd be so pro-
tective of—I usually end up welcoming her help. When I
get home at eight o'clock or so, my husband's usually just
walking in the door with groceries. She'll often prepare din-
ner for us while I tuck our son into bed. Sometime we'll
eat together; it depends what everyone feels like. Our
nanny's good at sensing—and I think we are, too—when
we all need a little time apart. She doesn't like to go out
much, but as soon as our son is asleep she retires to her
room with a book. Or my husband and I may head out to
dinner by ourselves. We've learned that if we truly want
to be alone, we can be—it just may be in public.

IN SEARCH OF PRIVACY

**When we're all home in the evening, we're on top of each other,
crowded into the kitchen or family room. I can't expect the
nanny to spend all her free time in her teeny little room—but
we need our own space, too.**

If you're going to have all the advantages of a live-in, trade-offs
are inevitable. You get plenty of freedom, but you also never really
get to be alone in your own house. The point is moot if you have
a nanny who is very independent and has a social life outside the
house—one who goes to the movies or to dinner with friends as
soon as she's off duty—or if she's happy hanging out in her room
with piles of books or magazines. Things can get sticky, however,
in the middle ground: You want your privacy, and she wants your
company. Reclusive sitters may need to be encouraged to venture
out in the evening with a few suggestions of what to do, where
to go. Some intervention on your part may help, such as pairing
her up with a friend's sitter. And it's certainly to your benefit to
have a car your sitter can use freely in the evenings, especially if
entertainment isn't within walking distance. In the case of a

nanny who doesn't drive, doesn't have friends or family nearby, and doesn't have any interest in going out, try to make her room as inviting as possible. Small as it is, there's always space for a VCR or boombox. And take comfort in the fact that, with experience, most live-ins learn how to "disappear" and how to make their presence scarce.

I'm sold on the idea of a live-in, except for one thing: I don't relish the notion of sharing the dinner hour.

Plenty of parents who were allergic to the idea of including the nanny at family meals find that an extra hand at the table can be really helpful—from managing tots to clearing plates. Still, most employers who want to, work out a way to keep the dinner hour sacrosanct—whether as family time or couple time. But if the sitter seems to be hanging around, waiting to eat en famille, then you have to be clear that when you sit down to dinner, she's out of the picture—and hopefully out of earshot. Try to set the situation up ahead of time; fill her in on the plan so she knows what to do with her time. During the day announce something like: "We're planning to have dinner around seven-thirty tonight with the kids." Or "we're going to eat late tonight without the children,"—adding she can feel free to have her meal anytime she wants. That said, life doesn't allow most families to stick by strict dinner schedules: Temper tantrums, play practice, forgotten groceries—all these interfere with the best-laid table plans. The best strategy is to stay loose and learn to live with the imperfect dinner hour.

I'm a private person by nature and I still can't get used to the idea of an employee seeing me in my pajamas or counting how many glasses of wine I drink.

There's not much you can do to avoid some level of exposure when you're living with someone under the same roof, unless you happen to have separate wings in your house. And it's not un-common to feel you have to be constantly on your best behavior, monitoring what you eat or drink, controlling your temper (fights with husbands, yelling at the kids). Of course, the reverse is also true—the nanny, as the employee, is probably doing a fair amount of keeping herself in check to maintain a professional exterior. In general, it's better to let your guard down a bit and avoid being self-critical about the way you behave in your own home. Employers of live-ins recommend you be yourself from the start. As in any relationship, if you present yourself as someone you're not, you'll have to keep up the pretense—and that can be enervating. No matter what, it's doubtful the nanny's keeping a ledger. If she's a seasoned pro, odds are there's not much she hasn't seen or heard before.

THE SEVEN-DAY-A-WEEK SITTER

We've always had live-ins, but only during the week. Now we're considering hiring a sitter from the opposite coast, who will obviously need to stay all seven days. It doesn't seem like there would be *that* much difference between five and seven days. . . .

A lot of parents prefer the five-day situation since it allows for a break in the routine and gives everyone a couple of days' privacy. With a seven-day setup, weekends are potentially awkward for everyone: If the sitter chooses to hang around the house on her days off, you may feel stuck with a third wheel, while she may feel stuck in limbo—she's not working, yet she's not really getting away from the job either. But there are also advantages to the seven-day week, the major one being that the sitter is on site, so you have more flexibility in terms of calling on her to help (on a Saturday night, say, or a Sunday afternoon). Whether you trade hours or pay more for the extra time, there's little chance you'll have to scramble for a last-minute sitter. With a full-week nanny, you also have the benefit of continuity; the kids don't have to go through that Monday-morning transition back to the nanny's care—nor do they whine and wonder where she's suddenly gone come Friday night.

THE SUMMER FILL-IN

Our family is planning to rent a vacation house for July and August, and our regular nanny is not able to join us. I've heard about summer-only live-ins—how and where do I find one?

The best candidate is a young woman who's got the time and interest to take on a summer-only stint—which often means a college student. Not surprisingly, employers who go in search of so-called American au pairs have the easiest time attracting women who live at some distance. The smaller the town you look in, the better, in some ways: You are more likely to find someone up for an adventure. A typical match might be a mid-western girl and an East or West Coast family living in an interesting city or summering in a hopping resort town. Some nanny agencies specialize in certain regions of the country—ask around to find which ones have which niche. The majority of parents, however, eschew agencies to avoid paying a fee for such a short period of employment. Instead, they recruit through word of mouth, canvassing friends and relatives who live in other states for names of local newspapers, so they can place their own classified ad. All of this is not to say you can't use those same tactics to find someone in your own backyard, someone who wants childcare experience and/or a summer break from her own family.

Overheard: The Mother's Helper with Caviar Taste

It was our first summer in the suburbs, and I hired a seventeen-year-old girl from Utah—a friend of my neighbor's nanny—to lend a hand with the kids for two months. She came with this amazing pedigree: Her father was a judge, her mother a pediatrician, and she was headed to Stanford in the fall. When I talked to her on the phone, I was thrilled she was interested in the position. Of course, what I neglected to ask was how she felt about hanging out in the backyard watching the kids jump through the sprinkler, or strolling into our little town to pick up new Play-Doh—which was pretty much the job description. From the get-go, she seemed bored and restless, plus she didn't want to do anything she considered beneath her, like take the garbage out. Not only that—we had a class problem, or so she thought. She was used being pampered and was accustomed to expensive things. She was condescending about the Ivory soap in the bathrooms, saying she only used milk soap from Switzerland, and cast aspersions on our generic sunscreen. She even criticized the car we gave her to drive (not up to snuff). At one point, she went so far as to describe our house as a shack, and then I lost it and found myself screaming, "Do you have any idea how much this house cost?" We sent her home ahead of schedule, and I promised myself the next time I hired a summer sitter, I'd care less about her resume and more about her enthusiasm for the day-in, day-out job of nannying.

WHO'S ON DUTY?

When I get home from work, the nanny is supposed to be "off duty," but she'll often hang out in the kitchen, and the kids

will continue to go to her with their questions and requests. I find the situation a little too nebulous.

Another parent may look at the same scenario and be thankful the sitter isn't taking off the minute the employer gets home—two ships passing in the foyer. Perhaps the stick-around nanny is trying to help you make the transition back into your home routine by not just dropping the ball with a clunk. Another possibility is that she finds it relaxing and enjoyable to be around the kids when she's not the one in charge. No matter what, if you're the kind of person who prefers a clear-cut deliniation between the end of your workday and the start of your parenting duty (and you don't like feeling superfluous), you have to come right out and say that when you get home, you want time and space to reconnect with the kids—without an audience. Be solicitous and enlist the nanny's cooperation in redirecting the kids' focus to you and your authority. Ask for example, "Will you help me by telling the kids that if there's anything they need when I'm here, they should 'ask Mommy'?"

Nanny Point of View: My Nights Are My Own

"One night I heard the four-year-old get up and run into the bathroom with a case of the stomach flu. It was about three in the morning and I could hear the mother comforting her. I didn't get up—in fact, I remember thinking I'd better get some sleep because my boss would really need me to be fresh in the morning. But the next day, the mother made some snide remark about how I must be a real sound sleeper. I didn't say anything back to her, but I felt her attitude was unfair. She's the parent, and it's only right that she did sick duty—besides, you don't need two people to watch a kid throw up."

SOCIAL LIVES

I wouldn't expect a live-in nanny to suddenly cut herself off from friends and family when she comes to work for us. But how do I handle "visitation hours" so my house doesn't get overrun.

This is one of those questions that looms larger in theory than it does in reality, and few parents find it necessary to establish rules. If you're talking about a socially active nanny, odds are she'll meet friends outside of the house. Even if you find yourself with a stay-at-home type, it's unlikely you'll encounter more than the occasional visit from a husband, boyfriend, sister, niece (such visits, by the by, help fill in the picture of your nanny's other life). And those nannies who go home on weekends get to see their family and friends then. If, however, you do find your house is turning into a central meeting spot—for other sitters and their buddies—then you're well within the bounds of employer etiquette to nix or limit visitors. You don't have to present yourself as antisocial—you could certainly shift the blame onto the size (if relevant) of your apartment or house, along the lines of, "I don't mind you having a visitor every once in a while, but the apartment is small and I'm not good with a lot of commotion—it makes me a little batty." A respectful nanny will get the message. If your house is big, there's a simpler solution: Have them stick to one area—the playroom or basement, or even the nanny's bedroom. Out of sight, out of mind.

Our nanny has a new boyfriend, and they go out every Saturday night. One Sunday morning, she came down to breakfast with him and introduced him around the table. We're no prudes, but we feel uncomfortable with the sleepovers.

You may not give a hoot who she has sex with, but it's understandable that you might not want to get into a discussion with your kids about who this guy is or the nature of their relationship. To her credit, a nanny who is up front about her liaison is not trying to sneak one past you. But a little discretion may be more appreciated than outright candor. You could simply request that her friend be gone very early in the morning, before the children wake, or insist that the overnights happen at his place, not yours—that is, if she can get back to the house by the time the kids wake up (a risky proposition). Some parents who have experienced the boy-at-breakfast scenario say that, morality aside, one of things that bothers them is being thrust into the role of parent to the "older adopted child," who is seeking approval of her latest beau—a level of involvement they could do without.

We have a young girl from Idaho living with us for the summer, and she goes out—and stays out late—a lot. I don't want to play her mother, but I do want her to be alert the next day.

While some employers have no problem setting a curfew for nocturnal nannies, the majority feel a tad uncomfortable about doing so, particularly if they were social animals themselves in their younger, less-encumbered lives (many parents, in fact, say they have trouble policing any kind of behavior they once, and not too long ago, reveled in). But no one wants a slug for a sitter who vegges out on the couch the next day instead of playing with the kids. To modify this "bad girl" behavior, start with the most benign approach: "Are you getting enough rest? You look a little wiped out." If she doesn't catch on, you could ask her to limit her nights out to those two a week when you don't need her to be "on" the next morning. If nothing changes, you've got a problem, and you'll probably need to deliver an ultimatum: Either she focuses on her day job or she's out of a job.

Chapter 15

Adventures with an Au Pair

She arrives from overseas with a suitcase and a desire to see America. She's young, eager, and about to join your family for a year. She's an au pair, which means "equal" in French—and in many respects, she's like an exchange student. In return for taking care of the kids, she gets room and board and what amounts to spending money. The family, for their part, is required to help the au pair find an educational course or two, and allow her to explore the social and cultural climate.

The deal is awfully tempting. After you pay the up-front agency fees, the average wage is $140 a week, roughly one-third the price of a full-time, professional nanny, and with no tax strings attached. The arrangement is totally legal, and there are no green cards to worry about (au pairs travel to the United States on a J-1 cultural visa, good for twelve months). That all holds true if you go with one of the six official au pair organizations, such as Au Pair Care and Au Pair in America, that are overseen by the United States Information Agency; if you choose to hook up with one of the many unofficial au pair services, some of which are no more than a one-woman, shoestring operation, you may pay a bit less, but be aware you aren't taking the legal road.

In exchange for a hefty finder's fee of a couple of thousand dollars, all of the official agencies, and many of the others, make life simple. They not only take care of all the paperwork, they also establish clear-cut rules about hours. An au pair is not allowed to work more than ten hours a day, for a total of forty-five hours per week, and she gets one and a half consecutive days off per week, with one full weekend off every month. And her sleep is her own; it's considered beyond her duties to get up at night to deal with a sick or scared kid. The au pair's not supposed to supplant the parents in any way; after all, she's barely out of her teens, if that.

The young age of most au pairs—we're talking eighteen to twenty-six years old—is something to consider, especially if you need childcare for an infant. While some au pairs come with rather substantial resumes (as counselors or student teachers), many have little or no childcare experience. In the wake of the "Nanny Trial," in which twenty-year-old British au pair Louise Woodward was convicted of manslaughter in the death of her eight-month-old charge, some agencies now require from two to six months experience for those au pairs who are placed in families with infants. The threat of neglect, ignorance, or violence aside, the majority of problems, say the agencies, arise from unrealistic expectations on the part of the parents, who give the young woman (or the occasional young man) the responsibility and workload of an older, professional caregiver. A family, meanwhile, may be surprised to find that they suddenly have another child, this one a teenager, on their hands, with all the attendant adolescent issues—from dating to drinking to the "what am I going to do with my life" blues, not to mention homesickness of the most basic and sorrowful kind.

As far as hiring goes, most agencies send a screener to your home to interview you and your kids, then have you fill out a background questionnaire on your family, complete with hobbies, photos, and daily routines. Typically, a few days later, the agency offers up an applicant—along with her educational info, essay, photographs, references (usually personal or school-generated)—for you to approve or not. The next step is a long phone call, in which you get to interview—and get to know—the prospective au pair as best you can.

Still, the prospect of hiring a girl you've never met to care for your children can be unnerving. And the highly divisive and provocative Woodward case hasn't helped dispel those fears. The trial tapped into every working parent's nightmare: That the stranger they've hired to care for a child could actually be a threat to their kid's safety. But, truthfully, even hiring an experienced nanny doesn't guarantee that she'll take good care of your child. And for all the scary headlines, there are thousands of success stories about au pairs, many of whom become loving companions to the children and continue to play a part in the lives of the families.

How contented you are with the au pair, and vice versa, hinges in large part on just that feeling of being part of the family. The arrangement seems to be most successful when the family extends itself, bringing the au pair with them on vacations, giving her perks like her own phone, TV, or use of a car, and actively encouraging her social life. On that score, she's going to want to go out in the evening and meet up with her friends, travel a bit, "see the world." Ultimately, being generous serves your own interest: A happy au pair makes for happy kids which makes for happy parents.

THE REAL DEAL

Full-time childcare for less than $150 week—it sounds too good to be true. There must be hidden expenses.

Yes, au pairs are a good deal—and yes, there are additional fees. Although each of the six official organizations governing au pairs calculates the expenses a bit differently, all the salaries plus extras add up to the same amount, give or take a few hundred dollars. Costs you might not have figured on include the application fee (about $100), the interview fee (ditto), the placement fee once you select an au pair (about $400), something called the arrival fee (about $800), the domestic airfare surcharge (from $100 to $300), an educational allowance (up to $500), and the kicker—the agency fee, (about $2900). Altogether, these add-ons total nearly $5,000. Looked at another way, if you spread the additional expenses over fifty-two weeks you're paying almost another $100 per week, bringing the real overall cost of an au pair closer to $250 per week. If you choose to deal with a smaller, unregulated agency, of which there are dozens across the country, fees tend to be a little less—though you also get fewer services. Any way you cut it, au pairs are a relative bargain when compared to the cost of a professional nanny, which can easily run twice as high.

We've had live-in nannies before, but we're about to hire our first au pair. Are we expected to give her all the perks—holidays, vacations, bonuses—that we've doled out in the past?

Not all—and you don't have to determine what she gets, anyway. One of the advantages of hiring an au pair is that you inherit the infrastructure—including the accounting department—of the agency, which works out all scheduling and money details, relieving you of that burden. Au pairs typically accrue vacation time at the rate of one day per month, starting the third month of their employment, for a total of ten days off per year. As a rule, au pairs don't get holidays off (save for Christmas and New Year's Day), which is relief for parents who find themselves torn over whether to grant the smallish holidays. And parents are off the hook when it comes to a bonus at Christmas time—most simply buy a small gift and call it done. But lest you worry au pairs are getting a bum deal, realize that they receive plenty of perks by virtue of their status as honorary family members—they travel with the family, eat out, go to shows, sports events, and weekends at the beach. It's all part of their social and cultural edification.

I've read that employers are required to pay for the au pair to take some sort of educational course. Is that real or bogus?

The requirement used to be pretty loose—an au pair could take the equivalent of underwater ballet or basket making and no one really cared. But the United States Information Agency now mandates that au pairs take six semester credits—and the agency has been known to poke around to find out whether au pairs are really satisfying the requirement. Parents must agree to chip in up to $500 for the au pair's education—a sum that doesn't go far. Very few four-year colleges or universities offer courses that cheaply, which means that the au pair is left with the option of a continuing education program or community college. While there's no approved course list, popular classes include computer science, child development, and—no surprise—English.

Au Pair Point of View: Out of Pocket Money

"There are some things about my situation here I thought would be different. I thought I would have a bigger room with a TV and I thought I'd have more free time. I also thought my pay would be enough to cover my expenses—now I don't think so. I have to buy shampoo and toothpaste; I have to pay my entrances to museums and cinemas; I have to pay for my phone calls. The money just goes."

Hiring and Acquiring

I've seen several ads in the newspaper for different au pair agencies, and they all sound essentially the same. Why choose one agency over another?

Your first decision is whether to go with one of the government-sponsored agencies or one of the countless home-grown operations. The advantage to going small is that the fees tend to be lower, and you're not dealing with a bureaucratic organization—and therein lies the disadvantage, too. Let's say you register with a teeny outfit run by one woman who's recruiting her cousins in Ireland—there's no guarantee the au pairs will be legal, and there's no organized support system for them once they're here. Most parents choose to sign with one of the six official American au pair agencies, which are alike in the big ways—they all require their au pairs to speak conversational English, have completed high school or higher education, be in good health, and undergo background checks. But there are some subtle differences between the agencies. Parents who are old pros at the au pair process suggest a few pointers that they learned the hard way: Ask about each agency's matching procedure—some firms only offer one applicant at a time, others suggest several for you to choose among; meet with each coordinator in your region (agencies will send them to you)—this is a person you'll be having at least monthly contact with after the au pair arrives, and whom you'll call with problems; you may hit it off better with one than another. Also, ask how many families and au pairs that coordinator is responsible for; obviously someone who's looking after sixty families will have less time and energy for your concerns than one who's supervising only ten.

I keep hearing about illegal au pairs—girls you hire directly from a foreign country through newspaper ads or friends who live overseas. What's the story and what's the risk?

There's much more downside than upside in hiring through the back door. The biggest being, If it doesn't work out, you don't have the safety net of an agency to fall back on—you're out there on your own trying to look for a replacement. And while it's not likely you'd get caught for hiring illegally, it does happen. Say the au pair gets in a car accident and the police get involved; they could well turn the Immigration and Naturalization Service on her—and you. The motivation for parents to go the illegal route is usually financial: They avoid paying all the agency fees. But they also bear the cost of travel expenses to get her here and back, as well as any medical costs. And they could end up bearing the entire psychological burden of her happiness, since the au pair could not turn for help to the counselors available through legal organizations.

Au Pair Point of View: Job Motivation

"I decided to be an au pair because I wanted to improve my English and see what America is all about. What I really needed was a year away from home to 'grow up' and think about what I want to do next." Although I like kids, I have no interest in making a career out of childcare—my time abroad served its purpose.

When the agency and I talked about au pair candidates, I was asked if we'd consider a young man. It hadn't even occurred to me there was such an option.

Although the majority of au pairs are still young women, there are increasing numbers of men who are interested in the child-care—and cultural—experience. Most families are wary of going with the opposite gender, simply because it's unfamiliar, but the feedback from parents who have taken on male au pairs (usually, and not surprisingly, to care for sons) has been very positive; agencies report few problems. (Of course, this may be just a co-incidence of numbers since there are so few men in the field.) On the surface there's no reason to reject the option of a male au pair; an au pair is not intended to be a surrogate mother, but another set of hands around the house. And a young man can just as easily drive a car, make a sandwich, play tag, and dial emergency numbers.

We're interested in hiring an au pair in large part because we want our kids, who are three and five, to be exposed to a second language—preferably French. Can we request an au pair from France or Switzerland?

Request yes, demand no. As much as an agency will want to please you, they can only offer up the candidates they have in their queue. As for the French-tutor scenario, it goes against the U.S. governing body's mission statement. A primary goal of the program is to provide the opportunity for au pairs to immerse themselves in all things American; the host family is to offer them an atmosphere in which to practice their English skills, not vice versa. That rule doesn't always translate literally in the real world, of course. Lots of parents have been known to arrange tutoring sessions without the agency's knowledge, for which they pay their au pairs an extra hourly wage.

Overheard: The Big Disappointment

I hadn't had much luck finding au pairs through word of mouth, so I decided to go the straight agency route and pay the fees. The agency presented us with an au pair they called their "best Irish girl." She came with stellar references, a degree in psychology, pictures of a lovely family, stories about nephews and nieces that she cared for. Not only was she charming to talk to on the phone, the previous family she'd babysat for gave her the most glowing recommendation I'd ever heard. Contrary to all expectations, she turned out to be lazy and irresponsible. Every time she was supposed to be home, she said she was stuck in traffic or held up at the doctor's. She was always getting headaches, neckaches, or stomachaches. And she lied all the time: I thought she was going to school two days a week; instead, she was hanging out with friends in town. When I'd had it, I called the agency. They were surprised, but arranged for a replacement who was a vast improvement. What I learned is the agency is no guarantee. Finding a good match is still a matter of good luck.

THE LONG-DISTANCE INTERVIEW

I can't imagine hiring someone halfway across the world to come here and live with us sight unseen. How do you get to know a person in one phone call?

You don't. Most seasoned au pair employers recommend two or three conversations before you make a final decision, to allow your thoughts and second thoughts a chance to brew. These parents also recommend that you let the conversation ramble on for forty-five minutes or so, to get beyond the routine questions and the scripted responses. Ask the kinds of questions that elicit revealing answers. Have her, for instance, describe the children she's taken care of; you may get a feeling for the ages or types of kids she feels most confident with. Ask how her family and friends feel about her being an au pair; will they urge her to hang in there when she calls home heartsick? And throw out a question like: What does she think she'll most look forward to about going home when her year is up; if she can't think of a thing, that's a possible red flag that she's seizing this opportunity as a one-way ticket out of her present life. We've all heard of au pairs who come in search of a career in modeling or a green-card bearing, wealthy husband. Such missions are distasteful to some parents, inconsequential to others.

Overheard: Up Close and Personal

When I first considered using an au pair, I couldn't get comfortable with the idea of hiring someone on paper or over the phone. So once we decided to give the program a try, I flew to Paris to meet the candidate I had interviewed and liked on the phone. The agency thought I was crazy, my husband thought it was overkill, but I justified the trip by figuring the cost of the program was so much less than we'd been paying for childcare, we could afford to do it. And was I ever glad we did. That wonderful girl on the phone was a nightmare in person—morose, slovenly, and slow, to the point that I could never imagine her throwing a ball and running around the backyard with our kids. I was only in Paris for three days, but I met several prospective au pairs the agency had on file—and found one I absolutely clicked with. We've now hired five au pairs this way; my husband and I make an annual trip of it—a long weekend in Paris to interview new girls and, while we're at it, take a little holiday.

After Hours

I have a twenty-year-old au pair coming from Hungary and already I'm worried there won't be much of a social life in our town. I want her to be able to meet people and have fun.

Families are usually spared the role of social director—that typically falls on the shoulders of the agencies, which seem to do a pretty good job. Au pairs in cities, suburbs, and small towns report they make lots of friends through regular "cluster" meetings; and often when a newcomer arrives, she's welcomed by girls who have been in the States a few months and know the ropes. While some parents worry that an au pair won't have enough of a social life, others fear the opposite: They'll inherit a party animal. And that does occasionally happen (remember the age we're talking about). How tolerant you are may depend on how much her rabble-rousing interferes with her ability to work the next day. If you find yourself with a sleep-deprived, bleary-eyed sitter in the morning, you'll probably have to lay down the law (going out weekends only) and she'll have to toe the line. Your leverage: A warning to her that she risks being bounced to another family, which may not be nearby (and near her friends), or saying au revoir to the States altogether.

Overheard: Partying Too Heartily

Our Belgian au pair exceeded our expectations—for the first four months. Then things started to slowly, steadily go downhill. She began treating my house like a vacation home—sleeping late, lounging around the pool, and basically doing nothing while I was chauffeuring the kids around. We went away for the weekend once and discovered she'd had a party in our house in our absence. Around the same time, she began coming home very late from her evenings out. My instincts told me she was drinking—but I didn't believe she'd drink and drive (in my car, no less). Then I got the dreaded call at three-thirty in the morning from the police station: She'd been going ninety-five miles per hour, swerving all over the road. We had to bail her out and go to court with her. My husband thought we should give her a second chance, but I was dead set against it. If she'd hurt or, God forbid, killed someone, I would have been responsible since it was our car and she was in our employ— and it could have wiped us out financially. As it was, she lost her license and all my trust in her. The agency found her another job, and the next nanny I hired was a straight-laced mom of forty-five.

Working on the Sly

I know that an au pair is only supposed to work forty-five hours a week but if she *wants* to work extra, is that allowed? And how much should we pay?

The au pair agreement clearly states a limit of forty-five hours per week spread over five-and-a-half days; this is to hedge against burnout and allow her time to pursue cultural and educational endeavors. But we're not talking law here. Overtime, at a wage competitive with those of nannies in the neighborhood, is often tacitly agreed upon between parents and au pairs. After all, the work is in the au pair's interest, who is almost always in search of more pocket money. Occasionally, au pairs will start showing interest in earning extra bucks by babysitting for other families around town. While the additional work is good for her wallet, it may make her tired or grumpy, which doesn't pay off for you and your kids.

Our au pair has a lot of time on her hands while my three kids are all in school. It seems crazy not to have her help me out around the house, but how much can I expect?

Not much. The responsibilities of an au pair, carefully prescribed by the agency, are limited to preparing the children's meals, making the children's beds, doing the kids laundry and straightening up their belongings. Finito. In no way are au pairs to assume housekeeping duties. Parents agree to that limitation in concept, but day-to-day life is a different story. Certainly, it can be frustrating to watch an able-bodied twenty-two-year-old sitting at the kitchen table, reading a book while you're killing yourself to get the wash and shopping and cooking done. But remember the bargain: a live-in mother's helper for very little money.

THE PROBLEM AU PAIR

I've got a serious incompatibility problem with our au pair. We rub each other the wrong way in every way—and it's not getting any better. What's our recourse?

Replacing an au pair is possible, but complicated. Most agencies offer "return policies" within the first sixty days, without a lot of questions asked. After two months it's still possible to do an exchange, though you have to prove some pretty extreme behavior. In either case, the agency has to find a new spot for the woman you want to dump, which can take a few weeks. Plus, they've got to hook you up with someone new, which can take even longer. All the while, of course, the disgruntled au pair is still boarding with you, continuing to care for your kids, eat your food, and drive your car, all of which can be awkward and unpleasant. And then there's the timing of the visa: It's unlikely that you'll find a new au pair with exactly the same amount of time left on her visa—whether it's ten months or two. Agencies handle any overlap by asking parents to pay an additional monthly fee for any time that extends your year-long agreement.

THE LOVE AFFAIR

Our whole family has come to adore our au pair, but unfortunately her year is almost up. I wonder if there's anything we can do so that she can stay on?

While there's nothing one can do legally, au pairs and parents sometimes circumvent the law: The au pair leaves the country once her stint is over—only to make a quick U-turn and come back with a tourist or student visa (both of which prohibit her from earning money while here and are good for only three months). Even though this plan works in terms of getting your irreplaceable au pair back, there's uncertainty and risk involved— if she needed to return to her home country for any reason, she wouldn't be able to get back into America because her visa would most likely have expired. The other downside of renewal is more emotional. Given the age of au pairs, most parents report that there's a natural arc to the experience: It seems that after a year of taking care of someone else's kids, the young women start losing interest and patience with the job—at that point they're ready to get on with their own lives.

Overheard: Marrying into the Family

Our first au pair left six years ago, but she's never gone out of our lives. The year she worked for us, we developed a very easy-going, natural friendship. Everything fell into place. She'd join us for dinners, go on family trips, and watch late-night movies with my husband and me, the three of us sitting around on a couch. Sometimes, when we'd have dinner parties at our house, we'd invite her to come. At one of these dinners she met a man, a friend of ours, who she began dating and later married. Our kids went to the wedding. Now she lives not too far away, and we still see her and her new family a few times a year. We've had four other au pairs since, and none has come close to our friend. I've never attempted to reenact the kind of intimacy we had with our first—I couldn't have. As I knew from the start, it was just one of those things.

Part VI

Taking Stock

Chapter 16

How's It Going?

Presumably, as with any relationship, you know when things are going well, when you need to work on a few areas, or when the whole thing's simply over. Or at least you think you know. In any case, it doesn't hurt to do a reality—or happiness—check, corny as that sounds.

A strong indication that everything's on the right track: You can't imagine how you'd get along without your nanny for one week, let alone the next year. Other clues: You wax rapturous about her to your friends, start every sentence about her with "we're so lucky," and—the real test—you wouldn't think twice about leaving your kid in her care if you were to go away for any length of time. If, on the other hand, you often find yourself fantasizing about the "perfect" nanny, or begin coveting your friends' sitters or reminiscing about your ex, it may be time to sit back, assess, and think about a change.

What if you don't feel one way or the other? There's nothing *wrong* with the sitter or the situation, but you're lukewarm about it all. Sometimes just okay is perfectly fine, and it's a matter of getting your priorities straight. Let's say the child is happy and well taken care of, but you don't feel *you're* getting enough pampering and perks. If that's the case, pause before switching sitters—it may be more important for the child to have the continuity of the same caregiver. But at the point where you feel your kid isn't getting enough—enough attention, enough social or intellectual stimulation, enough basic loving, it's time to start looking.

What if the kids themselves voice dissatisfaction? That's a little trickier than assessing your own feelings and observations. Depending on the age and the temperament of the children, not to mention other things going on in their lives, the intrusion of a caregiver can be a difficult thing to accept. As long as you feel the sitter is making the attempt to connect, give the situation time. Sometimes a reluctant child will suddenly, after a few months, turn to the nanny and out of the blue say, "I love you."

And beware the grass-is-always-greener trap. You may be eyeing your friend's nanny, who's always cheerful, cooks wonderful meals, and is trilingual. But don't assume she's perfect. The nanny may have tics and habits that would drive you crazy. Parents often glorify their caregivers the way they brag about their children. And often it's the newish parents who are on only their first or second nanny who sound off the most. What do they know from comparison? Suddenly they've got childcare! They might as well kiss the ground their nanny walks on.

An infatuation or "honeymoon period," about two or three months, can happen even with jaded employers who hire someone new. After the initial getting-to-know-you, working-out-a-routine phase, if things are going smoothly, employers tend to moon over their new nanny. Remember, everyone's on best behavior at first. It can't last. There are bound to be conflicts and run-ins. These, in turn, can get ironed out. It's usually only then that everyone settles into a familiar and comfortable routine.

Time however, is, a good gauge of how things are going. After six months you should feel that you're able to get along, talk about issues as they arise, and think or at least act together constructively for the sake of the kids. And certainly, by a year you want to feel that you can trust your sitter implicitly in any number of situations, from nurturing a sick kid to keeping a family confidence. If certain problems keep recurring, or things that have been discussed umpteen times aren't changing, then you've got a pretty good picture of the way the relationship will continue. Don't fool yourself into thinking that things will get better.

The other party in the mix needs to be accounted for, too. A withdrawn or moody sitter may simply be unhappy in the job. If you sense something's bothering her, it's time to talk. The only way to know may be to come right out and ask, "So how do you think things are going?" If you want to formalize the talk, or talks, set up a monthly meeting (or weekly for that matter) to discuss "company policy" and give her a chance to air grievances. Something that's easy to fix maybe irking or weighing on her, perhaps some little task you've asked her to do. Maybe she'd like to cut back her hours, or she wants more money. In the course of even the most amiable relationships, there are bound to be little negotiations and adjustments all along the way.

THE HONEYMOON PERIOD

Our sitter started out too good to be true—coming in early, staying late, walking the dog. Now, after three months, she doesn't seem to have the same can-do attitude.

It's not unusual for a new employee to want to make a good first impression. It's not unusual, either, for the initial wave of enthusiasm to diminish slightly as she settles into a more realistic rhythm, in which there are great days and flat days. It's unrealistic to think she could keep that up, and, anyway, as long as she's still cheerful and doing her job (the job you hired her to do) you can't really fault her. If, however, you notice a sudden and dramatic drop in attitude—she seems unduly glum, moody, angry—

then something's clearly happened, job-related or not. As the boss, the onus is on you to bring the subject up—she may be too uneasy to broach a prickly matter at this early stage of the game—with one of those "is everything all right?" inquiries.

I didn't want to be too tough on our nanny and throw too many tasks at her right away, so when she started six months ago, I eased her into the job. Now that I'm increasing her responsibilities, she seems put out.

No surprise—she thought she had a pretty sweet deal. Many employers gloss over the less appealing parts of the job during the interview in an effort to attract the nanny they want—and assume that it won't be a big deal to increase the load down the road. But as a general rule, it's harder to add responsibilities than to subtract them. Be realistic: Can she in fact do more? Would you want to, in her shoes? If yes, then this is a good excuse to have a review, which at six months is perfectly valid. Use the discussion to talk about what you'd like going forward—including a rethinking of the expectations (and possibly the salary).

Nanny Point of View: Trouble in Paradise

"I thought my new job was going to be ideal. I had come off a position with four young kids and was burned out on intensive childcare. This job was taking care of a house with two easy-going older girls, and the thought of doing housework, with its low stress factor, was actually appealing. But a month after I started, one of the daughters became seriously ill. She needed to stay home from school and take medication that began to affect her mood, which became erratic—and she turned into my first priority. The happy family that

hired me was now a family in crisis. I felt sorry for
them, but on the other hand, this wasn't the job I
signed up for. I was thinking of leaving but my bosses
gave me a raise. I began to turn a corner myself and
began to get satisfaction from helping the child get
stronger. A year later, things aren't back to normal,
but they're better and I'm glad I stuck it out."

Is "Okay" Good Enough?

**Our sitter is perfectly fine. She's always here on time, the kids
get along with her. But I keep wondering if there's something—
someone—better out there.**

Here's a dose of reality: Occasionally you do meet a super nanny—
a sitter who's capable, intelligent, and doesn't seem to have a
cranky bone in her body. But in general, for every strength in a sitter there will be a weakness. Still, you don't have to settle for me-
diocre—and you know that's what you've got when you're
constantly thinking to yourself, "I wish she were more this and less
that," and her negatives overshadow the positives. Good, however,
is pretty good, and you know that's what you've got if you never
worry about your kids' happiness or welfare or, when you pay her at
the end of the week, you tell yourself this is money well spent.

Romanticizing an Ex

**I bumped into our old sitter in town a few weeks ago—and was
immediately reminded of how warm and tender she was with
our children. Our new sitter seems a little reserved by comparison and I'm feeling let down.**

Lots of parents get stuck on old nannies like they do on old lovers,
particularly their first. You may well be glorifying her, or that

period in your life—who knows if she would even make you happy now. As for the new nanny, she may simply need time to loosen up and warm up. Kids' ages, too, can have a lot to do with how much affection a nanny displays—for many it's easier to snuggle with babies than with wiggly, jumpy three- or four-year-olds. Before you get stuck down memory lane and start living in an "if only we were still together" fantasy world, remind yourself, this is who I've got here and now—and start living in the present.

Nanny Point of View: Employer Envy

"A lot of the nannies I meet in the park go on and on about how nice and generous their employers are. Mine don't talk to me much and they certainly never do anything extra for me like give me a ride home or a day off. I like the kids and I need the job, but sometimes I wish I got a little feedback or encouragement from my bosses."

THE NANNY–KID CLASH

Every Monday, when I say to my two-year-old son in my most cheerful voice that the sitter is on her way, he cries out, "No, she's not coming! I don't want her to come!" I wonder if I should replace her.

Don't assume your nanny isn't doing a good job, and that it won't get better. By the time many reluctant two-year-olds are three, they're jumping all over their nannies, saying "Don't go home." In any case, the I-hate-you syndrome is inescapable at some point in the nanny experience, just as it is in parenthood. Given a choice, kids will do everything they can to boot out the sitter in favor of a parent. (These same kids, once the parents are out of

sight, are usually perfectly happy in the nanny's company.) However, if you don't detect any improvement over the course of, say,
six months, and the sitter doesn't attempt to win your child's
favor, you may have a personality mismatch.

**Granted, our kids—aged eight and ten—are not going through
the most delightful stages. But our sitter has taken to making
snide remarks about how "tough" they are.**

No parents like to hear their child criticized—they go into automatic defense mode. On top of that, no employer likes to hear
an employee whine about how hard a job is. As for the sitter,
there are a couple of possible explanations for her behavior. One
is, she's unhappy on the job for some reason—and this may be a
roundabout way of telling you. Or two, you have an informal,
easy-going relationship and she feels free to gripe and joke, forgetting once in a while that you're her employer and the parent.
Either way, in going forward, remind her that the kids aren't
necessarily going to get less difficult. If she doesn't get along with
them—or even like them—you've got to be the toughie and dis-
miss her.

**It's been a year since I had a second child, and our nanny, who
started with us about the same time, favors the baby over the
three-year-old. I've seen it from the beginning and thought it
would change, but it hasn't.**

A nanny who's been with a baby since birth is going to have a
certain maternal attachment that will naturally go a little deeper
than the affection she feels for a toddler, who's more independent
and is going to take longer to win over. Also it's human nature
to play favorites. Some nannies clearly prefer girls over boys, not
to mention certain kinds of personalities, whether quiet or out-

going. If the older child expresses feelings of being left out, or the balance is wildly off, you have to say something to the nanny about making an effort to even out the attention. Often with time, a good sitter comes to share affection equally.

Overheard: The Birthday Message

I know this sounds trivial, but it really bothers me: Our caregiver has been with us for two years, and she has never acknowledged our son's birthday in any way. The first year I wrote it off. But with his second birthday, I knew she couldn't have forgotten because I talked to her about his party—what kind of cake to make, how many kids to invite. I was really taken aback when the day came and went without a card or gift. She did mumble happy birthday, but that was it. Here she was, such a big figure in his life, and we had both made a big fuss over her birthday. I tried to figure out why it rankled so much—it felt like she was saying that the kid and the job didn't mean much to her beyond the paycheck. Or maybe she assumed our son had everything a kid could want, so what could she possibly give that wouldn't look insignificant. I couldn't get past the feeling that she was making a statement of some kind. And while we never spoke of it, I never forgot it.

THE BURNOUT FACTOR

The nanny has been with us since our daughter, who's now seven, was a toddler. Each year we've given her plenty of incentive to stay—bonuses, raises, lots of positive reinforcement—but lately she seems distant from us and our daughter.

It may have nothing to do with you. Many nannies, like schoolteachers, prefer to work with certain ages—and once the kid grows up (and into another "grade"), the nanny may simply not have the right resources, interests, or skills. There's also a natural burnout factor, in which the nanny grows bored of the same scene year after year; after all, in many other occupations people progress to another department, office, company. And the ennui works in reverse—employers themselves can burn out from seeing the same nanny over and over. When you hit the descending arc of the natural life span—about three years—it may be time for you both to move on.

Our nanny started with us when she was twenty-four and full of ideas and enthusiasm. Now she's twenty-six—hardly over the hill, but she doesn't have the same sparkle.

It's not hard to imagine fizzling out a bit in this field. Caregivers are quick to point out that employers underestimate how exhausting taking care of kids can be, mentally and physically (think about all the parents who are wiped out after a weekend of watching their kids, and can't wait to go back to work on Monday morning). And for some nannies, especially for those in their twenties, being a caregiver isn't a chosen career; it's a stopgap job, like waitressing, that serves while they try to figure out what they want to do with their lives. Whether or not your sitter's lack of enthusiasm is her passive way of telling you she wants to move on, she's lost joie de vivre, and that means there'll be no joie for anyone.

Chapter 17

Changes on the Home Front

You've got everything down to a system: The schedule works, the household is hanging together, the kids adore the nanny. Then something happens in your personal or professional life that throws the whole childcare arrangement off track. You quit your job, you start a second career, you find out you're pregnant . . . In the nanny–family dynamic, you're all reliant on each other, so if one person in the group makes a move, the others can't help but be affected, domino-like.

Probably the most common adjustment families make is adding another child to the mix. What does the extra responsibility means in terms of weekly pay? There's no one formula, since every situation has its own unique characteristics, but you can't get around giving some kind of increase, considering that you're doubling (or close to) a sitter's workload—unless, that is, one of the kids is off to school five mornings a week. Starting school can bring the logistic challenge of an easier workday. Once all the kids are out of the house five days a week, parents don't need as much help, but it's tricky to scale back hours and reduce salary—and hold onto the same sitter. Plus, there are always those sick days and school vacations: Is one of the parents always able to stay home to take on child duty? And once school lets out for summer, the kid is home again for the next three months (barring other plans, like camp). Who's on watch then?

On a emotional level, too, parents may face a dilemma if they don't want to lose a beloved nanny who's been with the family a long time. A common solution is to ask the sitter to stay on in a slightly different capacity—as a combination nanny-housekeeper-cook or some version of that. Plenty of nannies, however, refuse to "change stations," saying that any work other than childcare is beneath them. In this case the situation is self-resolving; once you reach an impasse, something has to give, or she has to go.

An employer's job loss or new career can also throw a monkey wrench into a well-oiled machine. Any period of financial insecurity may call for a temporary reduction or suspension of childcare. Even if the nanny's hours don't change, she may pick up on your anxiety and begin to worry about her own job security. What if you begin working at home? The new setup may or may not affect how much you can afford in terms of salary, but it will certainly affect the household. Suddenly, you're around all the time, even if you're closeted away in an office. Children sniff out their parents just as a dog tracks down a bone. They pound on the door, whine, scream; kick—the disturbance is bad enough, not to mention your natural instinct to go comfort the child (or get him to quit crying!). And the nanny who's been used to running the house by herself all day suddenly has to adjust to a parent looking over her shoulder. House and "office" rules have to be established as well as new, if invisible, boundaries.

No matter how well you've got things worked out, life doesn't stop rolling along. Perhaps you'll decide to up and move—will you bring the caregiver with you? Short term? Long term? What about the breakup of a household through separation or divorce—are you going to reduce childcare hours or increase them? Share custody of the nanny? And don't imagine that the nanny is immune to changes in her own life. She decides to go to night school. Or her children from another marriage or another country come to live with her. Or *she* gets divorced or pregnant. Clearly, you can't prepare for the unforseen (and even if something *is* planned, you can't predict all the ramifications). Deals can be made, hours shifted, salaries tinkered with. And new nannies *can* be found. No family or situation is static; so you've just got to go, as they say, with the flow.

ADDING AND SUBTRACTING

I'm pregnant with my second child, and my first is only sixteen months, so soon there will be two little ones at home. Obviously our nanny's job will get harder—how much extra do we compensate her?

Generally speaking, a new baby brings a 7 to 10-percent raise in salary to cover the increased workload: double the laundry, two times as many baths, not to mention the added stress of twice as much crying and fussing. You can, however, defer the raise if you're planning to be home on maternity leave for several months, or intend to be the primary caregiver for baby number two. Once you're back at work or you're at the point where she's fully in charge of both kids, it's time to bump her salary. Share your intention with the sitter vis-à-vis a raise as soon as you have the baby, so the game plan isn't all in your head, and she doesn't think she's been forgotten in all the excitement.

Our youngest is about to start kindergarten, which means all three of our boys will be in school until three o'clock, suddenly freeing up the sitter's days. We're not ready to give up childcare, but it seems ridiculous to pay her to sit around.

The kids-going-off-to-school scenario can be tricky: Parents may resent paying an enormous price for what's essentially back-up help, so they often throw non-nanny tasks—cleaning, laundry, cooking—at their caregiver to "get their money's worth," which may or may not be received well. Some nannies, especially those who see themselves as childcare givers only, resent the onslaught of busywork. Others get bored with all the free time and welcome the household chores—though a good nanny does not necessarily make a good housekeeper. If redefining the role is not an option, see whether she's flexible about her schedule—maybe you can play with her hours. Have her start her day later and work later, and/or shift the bulk of the "unused hours" of the week to the weekend—Saturday afternoon, say, through the evening. If she's inflexible about any or all of it, it may be you've reached the end of the line with this sitter.

Nanny Point of View: The Other Wife

"My employer is suddenly a single mom—her husband left when the baby was seven months old. My role in the family has grown; my boss has become very dependent on me for reassurance that she's being a good mother. Sometimes we joke about my being "the other wife." She constantly refers to me as being part of the family, which makes me feel a bit uncomfortable. But then again, I am very emotionally involved with the family, and at this point, I'd do whatever I could for the child."

I'm expecting my third child. I know we should give our nanny a raise, but we simply can't afford to—neither can we afford to give up full-time help.

As long as she's making a good, competitive wage, and as long as you raised her salary after your second child, don't feel pressured to bump again. There's no rule that every subsequent child brings an increase; otherwise, a family with four kids would be paying forty percent more than a family with one. You have to take the whole picture into account—how long she's been with you, how much her salary has grown, how much time she spends with the older kids (especially if they're already in school), how satisfied you all are. Best to be very honest—tell her that you'd love to give her more money because she's going to have this new baby to take care of, but that you've hit the financial wall. Promise her something as consolation: A padded bonus at holiday time, a guaranteed raise in a year, or a few extra days' vacation—not the same as a weekly pay hike, but compensation, nonetheless.

Our caregiver, who's been with us for a couple of glorious years, threw me for a loop the other day when she announced she was three months pregnant. I'm happy for her—but selfishly speaking, I'm not exactly thrilled.

The pregnancy, in and of itself, may not be a problem, especially if this is not her first and she tells you she's worked straight through her others. If so, assume she can go right up to her due date without much interruption in your routine. But if she gets tired, needs to leave early, or skips days here and there, expect you'll feel the effects of her condition. As for maternity leave, six to eight weeks is standard in the corporate workplace—and it makes sense here, too. The big question is, do you pay? It's a case-by-case decision and it hinges on loyalty. If you're very attached to your nanny, and vice versa, the generous thing would be to continue her salary at half wage (or full if you can afford it). Of course, there's always the chance she'll change her mind and not come back—or come back for a few months and then throw in the towel, exhausted by looking after her child as well as yours. The truth is, that's a risk every employer takes in this situation.

Overheard: The On-call Nanny

My kids are now eleven and eight. Over the last five years, while they've both been in school we've tried various kinds of childcare to cover holidays emergencies and afterschool hours but it's hard to find somebody good who only wants to work a few hours in the afternoon. Last year we interviewed somebody we really loved, so my husband and I proposed a strategy to her—one that has worked out well. For the hours that the kids are in school, from eight until three, we pay a reduced rate (five dollars an hour rather than our usual ten dollars)—and then from three to seven when she's with the kids, she earns her full salary. She doesn't come in to work during school hours—she's free to be wherever and do whatever—but she must be on call for emergencies of any kind, including sick children, early-morning business meetings and so on. We provide her with a beeper and she's been great about responding quickly. Of course, this works well because she lives only twenty minutes away. And although we never asked her to, she'll often come in an hour or two early during slow weeks to help out with the laundry, which makes us feel that she's not taking advantage of the situation and makes her feel she's earning her retainer.

UPROOTING AND UPHEAVALS

We're knee-deep in a major renovation of our old house, and almost every room is in some state of disarray or utter chaos. My mother came by the other day and said, "If I were your babysitter, I'd quit tomorrow."

People who go through renovations are usually so focused on their own anxiety, they don't think about how it's affecting everyone else in the house, including the caregiver. Renovations stir up a certain amount of baseline stress—the cumulative effects of drilling, sawing, hammering, and all that dust can fray a person's nerves (not to mention any added tension between you and the architect or contractor, you and your spouse, you and your kids). The best you can do is tell your nanny how much you appreciate her slugging though this period, let her go home early when you can—and maybe even give her a bonus for being a good sport when the renovation is complete. One word of caution: Avoid using a nanny as an intermediary with the contractor, plumber, whomever happens to be traipsing through—you don't want her making the wrong call, and she most likely doesn't want the burden of that responsibility anyway.

We're heading to the suburbs from the city and have to decide whether to take our caregiver. The kids are very attached to her, and none of us really wants to start over again.

A lot of parents try to hold onto the nanny for the same set of reasons, and it often works out—for a few months, anyway. The hitches include the sitter's potential dissatisfaction with a long commute (which most employers pay for), and parents complaining that the nanny always heads off early to catch a train or beat the traffic. Before long, parents are often asking around for local help. Regardless of money or distance, moreover, grafting a sitter from one environment to another doesn't always take. Some people are simply die-hard urbanites. It may be easier to begin fresh with a new nanny in a new place. Even if she's from the city as well, she'll have no basis for comparing the old setup and the present one; everyone's starting with a clean slate.

We've moved from Washington D.C. to Seattle and have had to part ways with the children's longtime sitter. But since I

haven't found anyone new yet, and I'm desperate for child-care, I'm considering flying her up for a few weeks to help us settle in.

It's comforting to have someone who's familiar with your family and your family's ways when you're trying to set up house in a new home. And it may be comforting for the children, too, who probably miss her. On the other hand, rewinding the tape has its emotional pitfalls. If the kids have said their goodbyes and are reconciled to moving on, it could be difficult for them (and you) to have to go through the scene a second time. Plus, familiarity has its price: Airfare both ways, and if you're taking her away from family you'll probably want to—or even have to—pad her weekly wage by 20 percent or so to lure her to you.

We're planning to move overseas in three or four months. I don't want to say anything to our sitter yet, because if she were to start looking for a new job now, she might find one and have to start right away. I feel bad holding back the information, but I can't take the risk of losing her now.

Between your guilt and the logistics of planning a major move, you're going to have to tell her sooner rather than later. She'll overhear you making calls about schools or talking to realtors about appraising the house or apartment. And once the kids know, forget it—you won't be able to keep the secret. But you do have some leverage in getting her to stay: namely, money. If you can afford it, give her an incentive. Offer a guarantee of a three to five-week bonus if she's with you until the bitter end, none if she bolts. The logic of the goodbye check is that, like severance (which in essence it is), it will help tide her over until she finds the next job—and that certainly eases the conscience.

Overheard: The Transient Family

My husband and I and our two-year-old son were between apartments for several months. We'd sold one, and then the deal on our next one fell through. Since my husband runs a design business out of a small loft, we all camped out there in one room. The trouble was, we had to be up and out by eight in the morning, before his employees arrived, and we needed to stay out until six, when they left. This was easy for me, since I worked full time, but it was no small inconvenience for the nanny. She was a real trooper, taking our son to every play space in town and taking advantage of every playdate that came up. I kept her abreast of our real-estate search and told her things would change. One day, she said that it was getting hard on our son; I knew she was saying it was hard on her, too. She didn't have a place to put her bag or hang her coat, she couldn't reciprocate play dates, and the office was in nonresidential area, far from parks, playgrounds, libraries— she did a lot of bussing, cabbing, and walking. After two months of this, my husband and I decided we needed to give her some kind of combat pay. We considered increasing her salary temporarily but figured it would then be awkward to reduce it again later. So we gave her a bonus of a week's salary. It didn't make her days easier, but it made her feel appreciated, and she stuck it out until we did (finally) find a new place.

HOME OFFICE POLITICS

A few months ago, I started working at home in a spare room—which is great except that my four-year-old keeps interrupting me, wanting to come in and "play work." I find it frustrating that the sitter lets him disturb me.

She may not know what you expect. Working at home is a whole new set-up, especially if the nanny was used to ruling the roost in the parents' absence during the day. Now she's got to adjust, and so do the kids. Since a nanny is only as useful as you make her, you need to set up guidelines and stick to them, as in: "When I leave my door open a bit, I can be interrupted if necessary; when it's closed and you need to see me, call." (Many parents set up an intercom or second phone line for remote communication.) As for deciding when to disturb you, a nanny should use the same judgment as she would for a parent working outside the home—would she call when the child was cranky, or only if the child was running a fever? Of course, you need to do your bit, too—which is basically to stay out of sight so you stay out of mind.

Every time my one-and-a-half year-old daughter sees me go in or out of my office over the garage, she runs after me, screaming for me. I quickly close the door, but I have to endure her cries for ten minutes or more. It makes me wonder how good a job my sitter is doing that she can't keep my daughter engaged.

Once you leave your work domain, it's over. You're cooked. No matter how good a job a nanny does, once your kids see you, they'll come running. Try to observe how the sitter handles the aftermath. Does she attempt to distract and redirect the child to another activity or a different part of the house? Or does she apparently willingly, let the child bolt out the door or out of her arms? If the nanny's doing everything she can to no avail, a little covert operation is called for. To make it easier on everyone, some work-at-home parents devise escape routes—side door, back stairs, and even, if you must, a window.

Now that I'm working at home, my nanny is more or less privy to my whole day. Every time I go out to the gym or sneak out to an afternoon movie, I feel strangely guilty.

One of the hardest parts of adjusting to working at home after being out of the house most of the day is the feeling of being observed. This daytime self-consciousness taps into parents' discomfort about enjoying themselves or doing frivolous things while the nanny is running madly after the kids. Before, you probably assumed that your nanny imagined you were working hard every minute; in fact, she probably wasn't thinking about your day much at all. As long as she's getting her paycheck, she's not going to be preoccupied with the details of what you're doing to earn the money, even if it means you've got your feet on your desk.

When I worked outside the home, I had a picture in my mind of how the nanny and my toddler spent the day. Now that I'm freelancing from home, I see and hear a lot more—and it doesn't match up to my fantasy that they were always reading or singing songs together.

Rarely does reality live up to fantasy in any realm. Of course, parents who aren't home all the time are going to fill in the canvas with their own ideal images—particularly if they feel any kind of guilt about working or remorse at not being there to do the reading and singing themselves. They imagine the kids taking nature walks, not sitting in front of the TV. But feeling let down or disappointed by what you observe should lead to a conversation about what it is you'd like to see happen—and what the nanny feels she can realistically do (nobody can be creative and stimulating all day long). Since you are home now, you can be sure that all or most of your requests will be heeded—that's one clear advantage to being on the premises.

Chapter 18

The Breakup

As in any well-wrought story, there's a beginning and there's an end. A nanny comes into your life, and then she goes—sometimes after a short period, sometimes after what seems like a lifetime. Circumstances change, needs change. Or perhaps nothing changes at all, and one of you becomes bored with the scenery. Sometimes parents and nannies simply grow apart, even if such a thing was impossible to imagine earlier on, at the height of the relationship. The split may be mutual and amicable or messy and hurtful. In many regards, how the end of the affair plays out has to do with whether the nanny is leaving of her own volition or you're pushing her toward the door.

It goes without saying that it's easier to be the one who's doing the breaking up. Nevertheless, letting someone go can create its own set of stressors. Some people approach the task of firing in a very matter-of-fact way, without a trace of self-incrimination; for many others, the mere prospect of breaking the news to the nanny causes them to squirm and prompts all sorts of avoidance tactics. Obviously, the tenor of the talk has a lot to with the motivation for the firing. If the reason is unrelated to the caregiver's performance—you're moving or all your kids are now in school—the conversation is less personal, and less charged.

But if you're switching sitters, the matter becomes more delicate. Many parents opt out of the direct route, using various techniques to ease the awkwardness. Classic chicken lines include: "We've decided we can't afford childcare anymore," or "I'm planning to leave my job and stay home with the kids." These fibs only work (and are only humane) if the nanny lives in another town and is unlikely to run into the replacement. Truth be told, a white lie has its place in particularly tense or prickly situations. Citing a rather insignificant, though not unrealistic reason for making a change—for example, "We need someone who drives" (or cooks, or can stay overnight, or whatever)—can provide the needed hook for letting someone go nicely.

No matter how you deliver the news you should give as much notice as possible, at least a couple of weeks—which is not to say those few weeks may not be highly uncomfortable, so much so that some parents simply cough up salary for that lame-duck period, and let her go. And as a rule, you should pay severance; the standard formula is one week for each year of employment. Of course, in the case of an abrupt dismissal carried out in a fury, you probably won't be feeling warm-hearted enough to give severance, let alone notice. No one's going to hold you to it, though chances are you'll reconsider the severance once you've recovered your composure and regained your perspective.

There's always the chance that the tables will be turned and you'll be burned—and often there's no way to see it coming (except maybe in retrospect, when you think back and pick up on the signs and signals). In the best case, the sitter gives you at least a couple of weeks' notice. But the quitting can happen without warning—a parent's worst nightmare. Here's the scenario: Everything's going along swimmingly, and then one morning nine o'clock comes and goes. Nine-thirty. You wait for the call from your sitter saying she's stuck in traffic or on a train platform.

Finally, at eleven, you panic. Something must have happened to her—or what? The "or what" might be that she's simply decided not to come to work anymore. Your day, week, and life, it seems at the moment, are completely messed up.

Whichever way it happens, a parent is bound to feel dumped. Or duped. But in the midst of your misery, if you can muster the will, it behooves you to find out why the nanny's leaving. Is she accepting another job for more money? Maybe she'll be wooed back with a matched salary or reduced workload. Or perhaps the solution is as simple as making amends, in the event that, unwittingly or insensitively, you said something insulting. Even if she's adamant about going, an "exit interview" is not a bad idea. Ask the nanny what went wrong; what you, as the employer, could have done differently. She's likely to be candid since she's got one foot out the door and probably has the next gig lined up. Why not gain something from the experience—a little extra insight for the next go around.

LEFT HIGH AND DRY

I still can't believe it: I was waiting for my live-in to show up Monday morning after she'd spent the weekend with her own family—but she never arrived. By noon I realized something was up. I went into her room and saw that she'd cleared out. No phone call, no note, no nothing.

This scene happens more than you'd think, especially on a Monday, when a sitter's been paid up through the week. And it almost always knocks the wind out of the parents. There are many possible explanations for the disappearing act. A nanny may have received a better job offer and feels too guilty or embarassed to give proper notice; she may have gotten herself into some kind of trouble, legal or otherwise; or she may simply be miserable in your employ and wants to avoid a messy scene. One could say, if it's any consolation, that if a sitter has the ability to cut and run, then she's doing you a favor by getting out of your life sooner rather than later. As with any kind of breakup, once you get a little distance from the dumper, you'll probably be less hurt and more relieved.

Nanny Point of View: Why I Walked

"The only time I ever up and quit a job without notice was when I worked for a woman who had a drinking problem. I couldn't stand being around her and dealing with her. And although I thought her husband was a nice man and a great dad, I wanted out. I didn't know how to tell her why I was leaving, so I just left on a Friday and later wrote the kids to say I needed to go for my own reasons, and that it had absolutely nothing to do with them. No one in the family ever talked about the mother's alcohol problem—and I wasn't about to be the first one."

Our new sitter had been with us one fabulous week, then out of the blue she told us she'd accepted a higher-paying job, and her new employers wanted her to start tomorrow. What went wrong?

Money talks, and if she's got a family to support, you can bet a nanny's going to go with the better situation, especially if she has no long-term loyalty to you. If she didn't even give you a chance to match the salary, there's a strong possibility the job holds other attractions, such as fewer kids, a bigger house, an easier commute. Sometimes the writing is on the wall—especially if the nanny took the job with you at a slightly lower salary than she came in asking for. The only way to hedge against this happening in the future is to either meet the next nanny's asking price or, if you offer her less and she takes it, to listen for hints of restlessness—at least you'll be heads-up to a possible problem.

Overheard: An Orchestrated Goodbye

Our first nanny stayed with us a year, much of which to my mind was perfect. Toward the end of the year, however, she began having trouble with her teen-age son, who was hanging with the wrong neighborhood kids and staying out all night. After a couple months of confiding in me about the problem, she told me she'd reached a decision: She was going to leave for a month to take her son back to live with relatives in St. Kitts, where they're from, because she couldn't handle him anymore. Before she left, she set me up with a fill-in—a friend of hers. She promised she'd be back in a month, but four weeks went by, then four more. Meanwhile, her friend said she hadn't heard from her either. Eventually the nanny called. She was back in the States—but she wasn't coming back to work; she said she and her husband were going to try to have a baby. I didn't buy the story completely. Why wouldn't she work while she was trying to conceive—didn't she need the money? Her friend continued to work for us, and she was nice enough, but not in the same league. Later we learned that our first nanny had gone to work for someone else, that her son had never left the country, and that she certainly wasn't pregnant. I was hurt, but in time I began to see her as deceptive and manipulative. And while she was a wonderful first nanny for our son, I wouldn't want her in our lives again.

THE EXIT DOOR

I've decided I want to let our sitter go, but I can't bring myself to do it. I'm new at this—and I'm bad at this.

A lot of people are cowards when it comes to the dismissal, and try to slough the job off on to a mate—who ideally is more comfortable with confrontation. Much of the fear of firing comes from the unknown reaction—will she get furious? Cry? Storm out? (Even if you suspect the worst, it's a total cop-out to do the dismissing via mail or answering machine.) When the reason for letting a sitter go isn't performance-related—you need fewer days or more housekeeping—then she's unlikely to take the firing personally. But if you're firing for more sticky reasons—she's never warmed up to the kids or she's cutting corners with the cleaning—then keep it short. Veteran ax-givers recommend that you not try to justify or explain away your decision, which may only invite her to defend herself, but present the decision as a fait accompli—for example, "This situation isn't working out, we've decided to make a change." The swift dismissal saves both of you from a protracted squirm session.

I'd been thinking for a long time about changing sitters, and I recently met a nanny who's interested in the job—but can't start for two months. I haven't said anything to our current nanny because I don't want her to bolt, but she keeps pressing me about vacation plans and I'm beginning to feel guilty about holding back.

In a way, it's a lose-lose proposition. By telling her now that you're going to make a change, there's a good chance she'll walk out the door in a huff; even with lots of notice and the promise of severance, some people react out of hurt feelings. By telling her late in the game, when she's already made her travel plans and maybe bought a nonrefundable plane ticket, you risk feeling like a double heel in that you screwed her twice. However bad you feel, the situation is still lousiest for her. Better to be a good egg: Tell her now and give her time to find another job.

Nanny Point of View: Changing of the Guardian

"I had a great interview with the young parents of a little boy, who lived in a beautiful apartment on the park. They asked me to start the next week. They also asked me to come in over the weekend so that the nanny who was leaving could show me around the apartment and the neighborhood. What I learned was a lot more than where to pick up diapers; she gave me an earful about the parents. The father, she said, was rude and the mother had a terrible temper. By the time my afternoon was over, she had convinced me not to take the job. I'll never know if the nanny was spreading poison out of spite because she'd been fired, or if she really saved me from an awful experience. But the risk of getting involved with mean employers was just too scary. I quit before I started."

I fired my nanny last night in a fit of anger and woke up with regrets. How do you unfire someone?

It's tricky, but it's sometimes doable if you're willing to grovel a little (apologies, apologies). Before you jump to put everything back as it was, however, stop and think for a moment. Usually when people are driven to fire an employee, it's not over one isolated offense, but rather over a string of events or an increasing feeling of disappointment and disillusionment. And often the remorse they feel has more to do with the failure of a relationship than with losing that particular person. It often happens that you take someone back only to have another major blowup and breakup. If you think that might be the case, stick to your in-the-heat-of-the-moment instinct, no matter how ill-considered it seems or how sorry you feel the morning after.

Overheard: The Serial Boss

I have a friend who couldn't hold on to a live-in nanny. She'd fired four in the last year alone, all for supposedly legitimate reasons. While she was between sitters she'd fly her mother into town to help out. She told me no one could care for her kids like their grandmother could. I'd met all her nannies, and they all seemed competent and caring. My guess was she couldn't hold on to them because she has too high standards—the no-one-can-match-my-mother syndrome—and also because she's a drama queen who gets a charge out the flare-up and the denouement of a good argument. Aside from the nannies, the ones who were suffering from her histrionics were her two kids, who had to get to know and then let go of one caregiver after another. What finally changed things was that my friend developed a side interest—a big one—when she and a partner opened up their own cosmetics boutique. Suddenly, her latest in a string of flawed nannies became perfectly acceptable— luckily for the kids, who've now had the same nanny for a record two years.

PARTING TERMS

We've come to end of the road with our nanny and have decided to let her go. Obviously, we're not running a corporation here, so what's the deal with severance?

The standard canon: One week for every year (or thereabouts) of service, given as a lump-sum payment on her last day. Depending on the reason for letting her go, you can adjust the figure up or down. Obviously if the nanny stole from you, mistreated your child, or out-and-out lied, then it's hard to justify giving anything extra. But in the majority of cases, when the partings are reasonably amicable, severance is the right thing to do. Exit pay is really meant to cover the unemployed person while she's looking for another job, at least for a couple of weeks. Of course, that doesn't guarantee she won't find new employment the day after leaving you, in which case the money is still hers—and that's life.

My nanny decided to leave the caregiving field for a job as a medical technician, and she gave me two months' notice, which I really appreciate. Since she's leaving us, am I expected to give her any kind of severance?

Quitting, unlike firing, comes with no severance obligation on your part. But if she's leaving on good terms and she's been kind enough to give you ample time to find a replacement, then a goodbye gift—on average about half a week's salary or the equivalent in a present—is appropriate. And if you think you want to continue a relationship with an ex-nanny for the occasional evening or weekend babysitting, you've got added incentive to give her a nice send-off.

We're reluctantly letting our longterm sitter go. She was sixty when we hired her to care for our newborn twins. And now that they're ten, it's hard for her to keep up. Severance per se doesn't seem to cut it—she's been like a member of our family.

Given the short-term nature of most sitters' employment, the "retirement package" is a uncommon phenomenon. But parents who feel particularly attached to their near and dearly departing nannies often give as much as they can. The main motive for your generosity is probably guilt over the fact that you're taking away her income and, given her age, it's unlikely she'll find work easily. Parents have been known to go as high as a thousand dollars per year of employment—or roughly double or triple the standard severance. Think of the payment as a combination severance and pension fund—and if you've been paying off the books and the sitter has no security (social or otherwise) to speak of, she'll need money more than ever.

Our nanny's leaving at our behest, and she asked me if we'd give her a good reference. I said sure, but obviously I have some reservations.

When a nanny leaves your employ, don't assume that's the last you've heard of her. Requests for references can dog employers for months or even years. A lot of parents feel responsible for the nanny's unemployment, so they soft-pedal their criticism, leaving out the bad parts and pumping up the good to prospective employers. But put yourself on the other end of the phone. Wouldn't you want complete candor? Instead of trying to save the sitter's skin, think of the kids who will be under her care.

THE LONG GOODBYE

Our beloved nanny left after five years with the family. While it's nice that she calls every week to say hi, it makes the kids miss her terribly.

Parents and sitters frequently keep in touch with one another, especially during the first six months after the split; then the contact usually drops off to a once-a-year birthday card or holiday call. In general, parents report that some sense of ongoing connection is healthy; it helps kids realize that the caregiver's affection wasn't based purely on the job. Lack of communication, on the other hand, often leaves a void that's hurtful, even to parents—it's as though the nanny has dropped out of their lives like a stone. But in some cases, keeping in touch can be too much of a good thing for the kids, who get upset at hearing the sitter's voice and hang up wondering why she can't simply come back the next day. Nannies who can't let go don't help the situation. Sometimes parents will intervene and ask the former nanny to limit calls to every few months—explaining that the children are still very attached and vulnerable, which should appeal to her caring, protective instincts.

Overheard: Ties That Bond

My daughter is nearly eleven and hasn't had a full-time nanny in almost three years. But the last woman who cared for her seems to have left an indelible mark, even though contact has been sporadic. Sometimes, when my daughter's feeling a little blue, she'll bring up the nanny by name. And on a few occasions, when she's been really upset about something—a fight with a friend or not making the gymnastics team—she's asked to call the nanny. Somehow, just hearing the nanny's voice, which we all remember as soft and musical, makes my daughter feel better. They obviously bonded in a very natural, familiar way during the two years they were together. The nanny saw our child in all of her moods, in all of her states of dress and undress; she cared for her when she was covered with chicken pox, and watched her perform her crazy dance routines. Who else, besides parents, can kids be so uninhibited in front of and feel so comfortable with? All my early-motherhood doubts about having a nanny versus doing it all myself left long ago. I can see that the caregiver didn't crowd me out. For this particular person, my daughter carved another place in her heart.

Appendix

AU PAIR AGENCIES

Educational Foundation for
Foreign Study (EF Au Pair)
One Memorial Drive
Cambridge, MA 02142
Tel: 617-252-6056;
800-333-6056
Web: www.efaupair.com

Eurapair Intercultural Child
Care Programs
250 North Coast Highway
Laguna Beach, CA 92651
Tel: 714-494-5500;
800-333-3804
Web: www.eurapair.com

Ayusa International
(Au Pair Care)
One Post Street
San Francisco, CA 94104
Tel: 415-434-8788;
800-428-7247

American Institute for Foreign
Study (Au Pair in America)
102 Greenwich Avenue
Greenwich, CT 06830
Tel: 203-869-9090;
800-727-2437
Web: www.aifs.com

Interexchange Au Pair
161 Sixth Avenue, 13th floor
New York, NY 10013
Tel: 212-924-0446;
800-287-2477
Web: www.interexchange.org

Exploring Cultural and
Learning/Au Pair Registry
6955 Union Park Center,
Suite 360
Salt Lake City, Utah 84047
Tel: 801-255-7722;
800-547-8889
Web: www.childcrest.com

Index

About the Authors

SUSAN CARLTON (*left*) is freelance writer who lives in Cape Elizabeth, Maine, with her husband and two daughters. Currently a contributing editor for *Mademoiselle*, she has written for a variety of magazines, including *Parents, Parenting, Self*, and *Mirabella*.

Photo by Ralph Carlton

COCO MYERS (*right*) is a freelance writer who lives in East Hampton, New York, with her husband and two sons. Currently a contributing writer for *Elle*, she has worked as an editor and writer at a number of magazines, including *Mirabella, Allure*, and *Self*.

Photo by Daniel Rowen